The Crusader States and their Neighbours

The Crusader States and their Neighbours, 1098–1291

P. M. Holt

Pearson Longman

Harlow, England • London • New York • Boston • San Francisco • Toronto
Sydney • Tokyo • Singapore • Hong Kong • Seoul • Taipei • New Delhi
Cape Town • Madrid • Mexico City • Amsterdam • Munich • Paris • Milan

Pearson Education Limited

Edinburgh Gate
Harlow CM20 2JE
Tel: +44 (0)1279 623623
Fax: +44 (0)1279 431059
Website: www.pearsoned.co.uk

First edition published in Great Britain in 2004

ISBN 0 582 36931 2

British Library Cataloguing in Publication Data
A CIP catalogue record for this book can be obtained from the British Library

Library of Congress Cataloging in Publication Data
A CIP catalog record for this book can be obtained from the Library of Congress

10 9 8 7 6 5 4 3 2 1

Set in 10.5/13pt Galliard by 35
Printed in Malaysia

The Publishers' policy is to use paper manufactured from sustainable forests.

CONTENTS

NOTE ON TRANSLITERATION

Arabic personal and place names follow the system used in the *Encyclopaedia of Islam* (English edn., 11 vols, Leiden: Brill, 1960–2002) with the exception of the following:

jīm is here transliterated j (not dj)
qāf is here transliterated q (not ḳ).

Turkish personal and place names are given in the modern Turkish orthography. The following should be noted:

ç is the equivalent of *ch*
ş is the equivalent of *sh*
ı is described in the *Concise Oxford Turkish Dictionary* as 'between the *i* in *big* and the *u* in *bug*'.

INTRODUCTION

The geography of the region

The region of the Near East that was profoundly affected by the Crusades and the establishment of the Crusader states extended from Asia Minor in the north to the Nile valley in the south. Between these sub-regions lay the coast and hinterland of Syria-Palestine, which formed the actual site of the Crusader states. It is useful to sketch in outline these sectors of the region.

Asia Minor, or Anatolia, the peninsula lying south of the Black Sea, consists broadly of mountainous territory with lowlands towards the western coast and in the centre. The mountains become higher towards the east and the frontier of modern Turkey beyond Lake Van, and here are the headwaters of the Euphrates and Tigris. The lowlands are broken up by the courses of several rivers, among them the Menderes flowing into the Aegean, and the Sakarya and Kızıl Irmak, both entering the Black Sea. In the south-east of the peninsula two large rivers, the Seyhan and Ceyhan, drain the Taurus and Anti-Taurus ranges, and enter the north-east corner of the Mediterranean. Important cities in the period of the Crusades were Smyrna (Turkish, İzmir) on the Aegean, Nicaea (İznik) and Nicomedia (İzmid) in the north-west of the peninsula, Iconium (Konya) and Caesarea (Kayseri) in the interior, and Adana on the Seyhan.

While in the Crusading period Turkish was coming to supersede Greek as the principal language of Asia Minor, Arabic retained its almost universal predominance in the Nile valley and Syria-Palestine, despite a prolonged Turkish presence, especially in the latter sector. The geographical structure of Syria-Palestine is less complicated than that of Asia Minor. East of a coastal plain of varying width, the backbone of the territory is made up of an interrupted mountain chain running from north to south. Its northernmost block, the Amanus Mountains, is at the point of contact with Asia Minor, lying east of the Ceyhan and the gulf of İskenderun. South of the gap formed by the outlet of the Orontes (Arabic, Nahr al-ʿĀṣī) to the sea, with the city of Antioch (Anṭākiya; modern Turkish, Hatay) lying some 30 km inland, the mountains resume to form the background for the important port of Latakiya and several smaller harbours. Another gap, formed by al-Nahr al-Kabīr, allows passage between coastal Tripoli (Ṭarābulus) and Ḥimṣ in the interior, with the mountain block of Lebanon to the south. The next gap is the outlet of the Leontes (Nahr al-Līṭānī), lying between the coastal towns of Sidon and Tyre. Lower and more broken hills to the south cease at the great gap of the plain of Armageddon, the strategic importance of which in Near Eastern history gave rise to the apocalyptic expectation that it will be the site of mankind's last battle. The plain connects the Jordan valley with the sea at Acre and Haifa, the latter lying below the projecting spur of Mount Carmel. The Judaean highlands, the setting for Jerusalem, continue southwards to merge with the desert of the Negev (al-Naqab) and the mountainous tip of the Sinai peninsula.

To the east of this highland chain lies a deep trough, which constitutes the most northerly part of the Great Rift Valley. It contains in succession the courses of the Orontes, Leontes and Jordan, followed by the expanse of the Dead Sea. Southwards beyond this it continues as the waterless depression of Wādī ʻAraba to reach the gulf of ʻAqaba, the north-eastern arm of the Red Sea. The eastern bank of this trough presents less of a bastion in the north than does its western counterpart, although the ridge of Lebanon is confronted by Anti-Lebanon, and the highland country continues southwards. This territory is dominated by four cities that the Crusaders never captured: Aleppo and Damascus, the metropolis of the north and south respectively, linked by an ancient route passing through Ḥimṣ on the Orontes and Ḥamāh with its access to Tripoli and the sea.

West of the Sinai peninsula lies Egypt, the northernmost sector of the Nile valley. The country consists for the most part of a narrow cultivable strip along the river, supporting numerous villages and a few major towns, finally expanding into the fertile triangle of the Delta. This is delimited by the two branches of the Nile, which separate about 22 km below Cairo to reach the sea at Damietta to the east and Rosetta to the west. Westwards again of Rosetta is the historic port-city of Alexandria, which was the capital of Egypt before the Arab conquest in the seventh century. In the Crusading period the southern frontier of Egypt was the First Cataract of the Nile, with Aswān as the border town. South of this point, in territory now divided politically between Egypt and the Sudan, was Nubia, then consisting of two Christian kingdoms centred on the river. The northern kingdom, Muqurra, had Old Dongola as its capital, and its southern border lay south of the confluence of the river Atbara with the Nile. Its northern borderlands had long been open to Arab raids and settlement, and hence there was some degree of islamisation there. In the southern kingdom of ʻAlwa, which extended up the Blue and White Niles, the capital was Sōba, not far from present-day Khartoum. Although a tenth-century envoy from Fatimid Egypt to Nubia speaks of a suburb of Sōba inhabited by Muslims, these were probably merchants and their families. 'Alwa was not yet vulnerable to Arab conquest and settlement.

The historical background

At the beginning of the eleventh century, which was some ten lunar years from the end of the fourth Muslim century, two great powers were established in Anatolia and the Nile valley respectively. Anatolia consisted politically of the Asian provinces of the Byzantine Empire. Its capital was Constantinople, across the Straits in Europe, where it also had provinces in Greece and the Balkans.

After the death in 1025 of Basil II, one of the greatest and most powerful Byzantine rulers, a period of decline set in. Under his feeble successors the state lacked effective control, while rivalry and factionalism developed between the civilian, court-centred aristocracy of the capital and the landed military nobles of the Anatolian provinces. From the latter group came two military emperors: Isaac I Comnenus (1057–9), who was driven to abdicate by an alliance of the Church and the civilian aristocracy; and Romanus IV Diogenes (1068–71), whose overthrow was a result of his defeat at the battle of Manzikert by a rising great power in the Near East, the Seljuks under their sultan, Alp Arslan. Only with the succession in 1081 of Alexius I Comnenus, a nephew of Isaac I, did the Byzantine Empire begin to regain strength.

Alexius was faced at the outset with a disastrous situation. During the ascendancy of the civilian aristocracy, the old military system based on the tenures of a free peasantry had decayed. Power in the provinces passed to the holders of great estates, while the imperial army became increasingly dependent on the recruitment of mercenaries, including Normans, English (after the battle of Hastings in 1066) and Turks. These last came from the Turcoman tribesmen, who had broken through the Byzantine frontier defences after the battle of Manzikert and flooded into the heart of Anatolia. Turkish emirs also established themselves at Smyrna (İzmir) and Nicaea (İznik), which became the first capital of the Seljuk sultans of Rūm (i.e. Asia Minor), Süleyman (d. 1085) and his son Kılıc Arslan in 1092. These sultans and their descendants were a breakaway branch of the Great Seljuk dynasty to which Alp Arslan belonged.

Byzantium, the great power of the north, was confronted in this period by the great power of the south, the Fatimid caliphate. The Fatimid dynasty had its remote origin in an Arab faction (Arabic, *shī'a*) in early Islam, when the legitimacy of the caliphs to the headship of the Muslim community was challenged by rivals, who asserted that the rightful heads were ʿAlī, the Prophet's cousin, and his heirs by his wife Fāṭima, the Prophet's daughter. As time passed and the Muslim community became multi-ethnic, this political factionalism spread and hardened into religious schism supported by theological dogma. Thus the Shiʿa stood in permanent opposition to the majority of Muslims, the Sunni Muslims, who dominated a vast empire, which was ruled from 750 by the dynasty of the ʿAbbasid caliphs. They took their name from their ancestor, al-ʿAbbās, the Prophet's uncle.

The Shiʿa were however not all of one mind. Most of them traced the line of descent of their heads, the Infallible Imams, from ʿAlī to the twelfth Imam, Muḥammad al-Mahdī, who disappeared from history in 940, and they held that he would reappear at the end of time to restore Islam. Twelver Shiʿism became the state religion of Iran in the sixteenth century, as it is still today. A variant claim to legitimacy was made by a fringe group, the Ismaʿilis, in the tenth century. They ended the succession of Infallible Imams with the seventh, Ismāʿīl b. Jaʿfar al-Ṣādiq, whence their name. As time went on they produced numerous sects, and one of these evolved into the Fatimid caliphate. Its leader, ʿUbaydallāh, claimed descent from the Infallible Imams, and began a widespread propaganda against the ʿAbbasid caliphate. He finally established himself in North Africa, where he won acceptance and military support from Muslim Berber tribesmen. There in 910 he assumed the caliphal title of *amīr al-muʾminīn*, 'Commander of the Faithful', thereby asserting a claim to supersede the ʿAbbasid caliph and to rule over the entire Muslim community. In 969 Egypt was conquered by the Fatimid warriors, and the Caliph al-Muʿizz, ʿUbaydallāh's great-grandson, moved to Cairo, a new city that he was building to house his troops and be his capital, lying to the north of al-Fusṭaṭ, the first major settlement of the Arabs in Egypt.

The long reign of the Caliph al-Mustanṣir (1036–94) occupied most of the eleventh century and ended a few years before the First Crusade. By this time the Fatimid dynasty had passed its zenith. The vigour of an autocratic regime depends largely upon the character and qualities of the autocrat, and Fatimid history was no exception. Al-Mustanṣir was a child of seven at his accession. Three ethnic military groups came to dominate the capital: Berbers, Turks and Blacks (*Sūdān*) from the upper Nile valley. During his reign al-Mustanṣir accumulated a vast personal fortune, and he had a library of over a hundred thousand volumes. The Turks looted his treasure and destroyed or dispersed the manuscripts. Famine was widespread and plague intervened. At last in 1073 the caliph sent for Badr al-Jamālī, his governor of Acre, who had started his career as an Armenian slave. Badr came with his own Syrian troops, and as a military dictator restored order and prosperity to Egypt. Then in 1094 both he and al-Mustanṣir died. Badr was succeeded by his equally competent son, al-Afḍal Shāhanshāh, and al-Mustanṣir was succeeded by another puppet-caliph, the 18-year-old al-Mustaʿlī, who reigned from 1094 to 1101, and was thus an insignificant witness of the irruption of the First Crusade into his nominal possessions.

Between the two powers of the Byzantines and the Fatimids lay the debatable land of Syria-Palestine, rendered by its geography and population structure both arduous to conquer and difficult to hold. The decline of the ʿAbbasid caliphate from the middle of the ninth century and the fragmentation of the Muslim empire had left it vulnerable to attack from without and a prey to instability within. In 969 the northern city of Antioch was retaken by the Byzantines after more than three centuries of Muslim rule. Held by them until 1084, it gave them a foothold and a sphere of interest in Syria. In the south the Fatimids sought to extend their control into Syria, following here the two dynasties of autonomous Turkish governors, the Tulunids and Ikhshidids, who had ruled Egypt during most of the century from 868 to 969. Jerusalem, a city of great importance to Muslims as well as Jews and Christians, passed under their rule. They were confronted, as were the Fatimids after them, by a rival Ismaʿili sect which had its headquarters in al-Baḥrayn, and are designated the Carmathians. The Carmathian forces in Syria were finally defeated in 978 by the Caliph al-ʿAzīz (975–96), and withdrew after obtaining the promise of a large tribute payment. The ending of the Carmathian threat did not however mean that Fatimid control of southern Syria was easy. Beyond Tripoli their power was marginal, and as it declined the judges (*qāḍīs*) they nominally appointed became autonomous rulers.

A feature of this period in Syria-Palestine was the emergence of Arab tribal leaders as rulers of territorial principalities. The first of these were the Hamdanids, a family belonging to the Taghlibī tribe, supposedly of North Arabian origin. Two brothers from this family, Nāṣir al-Dawla al-Ḥasan and Sayf al-Dawla ʿAlī, became autonomous amirs of Mosul and Aleppo respectively. The rule of the Mosul branch ended in 989, but the second Hamdanid amir of Aleppo, Saʿd al-Dīn Sharīf (967–91), maintained his position by playing off the Byzantines against the Fatimids, whose suzerainty he recognised in 986. Like other Syrian Arabs of the period, the Hamdanids were inclined to Shiʿism. Under Saʿd al-Dīn's successor, Saʿd al-Dawla Saʿīd (991–1002), the precarious balance of interests was upset in 1001 by the conclusion of peace between the

Emperor Basil II (976–1025) and the Caliph al-Ḥākim (996–1021), and the Hamdanid dynasty of Aleppo was extinguished in 1004.

They were followed as rulers of Aleppo by Ṣāliḥ b. Mirdās and his successors, the Mirdasids, from 1024 to 1080, who also belonged to a tribe of North Arabian origin, the Kilāb. More immediately troublesome to the Fatimids, since they were established in Palestine, were the Jarrahids, who belonged to the South Arabian tribe of Ṭayyi'. Unlike the Arab state-builders in Aleppo, they were a nomadic group. The high point of Jarrahid importance was at the beginning of the caliphate of al-Ẓāhir in 1021, when their chief, Ḥassān b. Mufarrij, made a pact with Ṣāliḥ b. Mirdās and a third tribal leader, Sinān b. Sulaymān of the Kalb. They agreed to partition Syria among themselves, Ḥassān taking Palestine, Ṣāliḥ holding Aleppo, and Sinān having Damascus. A Fatimid army was sent out under a Turkish commander, Anuştegin al-Duzbārī, who was defeated at Ascalon on the Palestinian border. Sinān died shortly afterwards, and the two remaining allies were defeated by Anuştegin in 1029 at al-Uqḥuwāna near the Sea of Galilee, where Ṣāliḥ was killed. Ḥassān fled to seek Byzantine support in the north. He and his people remained as an irritant to Anuştegin in proximity to Byzantine Antioch and Mirdasid Aleppo. The relations of the three powers were both tangled and unstable, and in 1038 Anuştegin entered Aleppo.

With Anuştegin's death there in 1042 Fatimid power in Syria began to decline. The nomadic tribesmen of Palestine continued as before to ravage the settled lands, and in 1071 the Shi'i Fatimid government invited Atsız, a Sunni Turcoman tribal chief, to deal with the troublemakers. He did so, went on to establish himself as ruler of the territory, and occupied Jerusalem. Fatimid attempts to oust him failed; he took Damascus in 1076, and unsuccessfully attacked Egypt itself in the following year. Atsız now sought the help of Tutuş, the brother of the Great Seljuk Sultan Malik-Shāh. Tutuş had Atsız assassinated in 1079, and Jerusalem was then held by another Turcoman family, the Artukids, who were expelled by a Fatimid force under al-Afḍal in 1098. A year later the city fell to the Crusaders.

The Turkish phenomenon

The pattern of military and political relations in the Near East was profoundly and lastingly changed during the eleventh century by the irruption and mutual confrontation of two new forces: the Seljuk Turks coming from Central Asia and the Frankish Crusaders from Western Europe.

Turks had long been known in the Near East, and formed part of its permanent population. This had originally come about through the development of the Mamluk institution, a species of military slavery, which had arisen as early as the first century of Islam. The great early expansion of the Muslim Arabs brought them into Transoxania, the territory beyond the river Oxus. This was the borderland of the Turks of Central Asia, and Muslim generals formed Turkish bodyguards from prisoners of war and men brought to them by slave-traders. In course of time such military households came to form a substantial component of Muslim armies. Entirely attached to their masters, these Mamluks were more loyal and dependable than freeborn Arab warriors, who were individuals with pride in their tribal traditions.

Preference for Turkish rather than Arab troops was clearly displayed when the ʿAbbasid Caliph al-Ma'mūn (813–33) included large numbers of Turks in his army, and pursued what was effectively a systematic immigration policy by levying revenue from the eastern border provinces partly in slaves. Al-Muʿtaṣim (833–42), his soldier brother and successor, continued to recruit Mamluk troops, and in 836 he transferred them en masse from the turbulent capital of Baghdad to a new city, 125 km north on the east bank of the Tigris. Samarra (officially *Surra man ra'ā*, 'he who sees it is delighted') consisted essentially of the caliph's palace and the cantonments of his Turkish troops, but it inevitably superseded Baghdad as the administrative centre of the empire and continued so until the closing years of the ninth century.

By that time the ʿAbbasid caliphate was in decline, but Mamluk households sustained the provincial governors and local rulers who had usurped power in all parts of the empire. The two gubernatorial dynasties in Egypt which have already been mentioned, the Tulunids and the Ikhshidids, were both of Mamluk origin. Aḥmad b. Ṭūlūn was said to be the son of a Turk who had been sent from Bukhara in the slave-tribute to al-Ma'mūn, and he went to Egypt as lieutenant-governor for his stepfather, a Turkish general. The Ikhshidids take their name from *ikhshīd*, an ancient Iranian title for a ruler. It was conferred on a Turkish general, Muḥammad b. Ṭughj, whose grandfather had entered ʿAbbasid service, and who was himself appointed governor of Egypt in 935.

Something must be said about the legal and social status of the Mamluks. The Arabic word *mamlūk*, meaning something possessed, a chattel, is synonymous with a term of more general range, *ʿabd*, which means a slave. The servile condition into which a Mamluk was brought by capture in war or enslavement implied that he was a pagan but since acquisition resulted in his conversion to Islam, he obtained rights as a Muslim under Islamic law, which moreover favoured emancipation on the death of his master. His religious status was theoretically the same as that of any freeborn Muslim. During the Mamluk sultanate of Egypt

(1250–1517), the completion of military training was automatically accompanied by emancipation. Thus the designation of the Mamluk sultans as 'the slave-sultans of Egypt' (the title of a nineteenth-century history) is doubly inaccurate: when they were slaves, they were not sultans; when they were sultans, they were not slaves.

The political and social stability of the Near East, which had long been used to Turkish immigration and settlement by the Mamluks and their assimilated descendants, was violently shaken by the irruption into the region of free Turkish nomadic tribesmen, the Turcomans, spear-headed by the Muslim clan of Seljuk. Such westwards movements of Turkish groups formed part of Eurasian history, and were sometimes catastrophic in their effects. The Huns were probably a Turkic people, whose devastating incursion into Europe culminated in the career of Attila (434–53). In the last quarter of the seventh century another Turkic group, the Bulgars, migrated from an earlier homeland west of the Sea of Azov and founded a state among the Slavs south of the lower Danube. This was Byzantine territory, and there were repeated wars between the two powers until the Bulgarian kingdom was overthrown and its land reannexed in 1018 by Basil II, known as 'Bulgaroctonus', 'the Bulgar-slayer'. Bulgaria had however served a purpose as a buffer state against another Turkic people, the Pechenegs or Patzinaks, nomads in the country between the Danube and the Dnieper. They in their turn threatened the territory south of the Balkans, where they established themselves in 1048. They harassed the Balkans and menaced the Byzantine Empire until they were defeated by Alexius I Comnenus in 1091. The emperor had been supported by another group of Turkic nomads, the Uzes or western Oghuz, who had pushed into the Balkans in 1064, pressed on by yet other Turks, the Kumans or Kipchaks, who replaced them in the steppes of southern Russia.

More will be heard of the Kipchaks, from amongst whom were recruited the founders of the Mamluk sultanate in Egypt. Of greater immediate importance was the much larger group of the eastern Oghuz. Unlike the other Turkic tribal groups that have been mentioned, they did not make their way westwards through the steppes north of the Black Sea but by a southerly route through Iranian territory. This was to bring them ultimately to the shores of the Mediterranean and Aegean. Their migration was, as has been said, led and to some extent controlled by the clan of Seljuk. Seljuk, the eponymous founder, lived with his people on the lower Jaxartes or Syr Darya, where it flows into the Aral Sea. On the northern fringe of Transoxania, they were open to Islamic cultural influences, and were converted to Sunni Islam in the second half of the tenth century. Local politics, wars and alliances brought them southwards into Transoxania and Khurāsān. The process of building a state on the foundation of their nomad warriors began with Seljuk's two grandsons, Tuğrul Beg and Çağrı Beg, who in 1040 succeeded in defeating the powerful Ghaznavid ruler, Mas'ūd, at the battle of Dandānqān, about 65 km from Merv in Khurāsān. The Ghaznavids were themselves a dynasty of Turkish Mamluk origin, and the second ruler, the conqueror Maḥmūd of Ghazna (998–1030), left to his son Mas'ūd a realm extending from the south of the Caspian Sea through Khurāsān and Afghanistan to the Punjab. His defeat at Dandānqān meant the loss of Khurāsān to the Seljuks.

Leaving Çağrı Beg in the east, Tuğrul Beg advanced westwards with his Turcoman nomads as they followed the grazing. The centre and west of Iran were dominated by an Iranian clan, the Buyids or Buwayhids, who also controlled Iraq and ruled in the name of the 'Abbasid caliph of Baghdad. This was an anomalous situation as the Buyids were Shi'is, although not of the Isma'ili sect from which the Fatimids had arisen. In 1055 the 'Abbasid Caliph al-Qā'im summoned Tuğrul Beg to liberate him from his Shi'i protectors. Buyid power collapsed, to be followed by Seljuk domination, and Tuğrul Beg was formally awarded the title of sultan, in Arabic *sulṭān*, originally an abstract noun meaning power. He was indeed the power behind the caliph's throne, and he now assumed the trappings of a Muslim ruler rather than the simple dignity of a Turkish tribal chief. The nomad warriors were supplemented, and increasingly replaced, by regular troops first obtained in Khurāsān, and the Turcomans were left free to penetrate westwards into Byzantine Asia Minor and Arab Syria.

Tuğrul Beg died in 1063, three years after his brother Çağrı Beg. He was childless, and the rule over the unified Seljuk dominions passed to Çağrı Beg's son Alp Arslan, who reigned from 1063 to 1073. He was a resolute warrior and a powerful sultan like his uncle. In 1070 he organised an expedition against the Fatimids, and advanced into northern Syria. There he heard that he was threatened in the rear by the Emperor Romanus IV Diogenes, whom he confronted at Manzikert or Malasjird, north of Lake Van, and defeated in 1071. The subsequent crumbling of the Byzantine defences in the east facilitated the immigration of Turcoman tribesmen into Anatolia.

Alp Arslan died of a wound in 1073, and was succeeded by his son Malik-Shāh. Perhaps to placate his brother Tutuş, who was a possible rival, Malik-Shāh conceded central and southern Syria-Palestine to him as an apanage. As ruler of this territory, Tutuş killed the Turkish chief Atsız, who, as mentioned earlier, was building up an independent principality around Jerusalem and Damascus. He extended his power into northern Syria by defeating and killing Sultan Süleyman of the Seljuks of Rūm (to be mentioned shortly) in 1085. As a result of this development Malik-Shāh came to Syria, where he confirmed Tutuş in his apanage, but brought northern Syria under his own control by appointing governors to Antioch and Aleppo. Yağısıyan, whom he installed in Antioch, was still there when the Crusaders arrived ten years later. Malik-Shāh died in 1092, and in 1095 Tutuş was killed in the ensuing succession struggle. His apanage, now to all intents and purposes an independent Seljuk principality, was partitioned between his sons, Dokak in Damascus and Riḍwān in Aleppo. Neither of them was completely master in his territory since both were overshadowed by their *atabegs*, Dokak by Tuğtigin and Riḍwān by Janāḥ al-Dawla. It was customary in Turkish principalities for a ruler's son to have an *atabeg* (literally, 'father-prince') as his tutor and guardian, who would become in effect the regent if the ruler died while his son was a minor. In these circumstances an *atabeg* sometimes legitimised his position by marrying the late ruler's widow, and might in fact found a ruling dynasty.

Alp Arslan's victory at Manzikert was the prelude to a process of state formation by two very different ethnic groups, the Turcomans of Asia Minor and the Armenians. Two principal families established themselves over the Turcomans. One was a branch of the Seljuk clan, the descendants of a prince called Kutlumuş, who had clashed with his kinsmen, the Great Seljuks, over the rule of succession to the sultanate. Süleyman, the son of Kutlumuş, took a part in Byzantine factional struggles, set up his capital in the far north-west at Nicaea (İznik), and was recognised as sultan of Rūm. He was killed in 1086 in battle with Tutuş of Syria, and his young son, Kılıc Arslan, became a hostage to Malik-Shāh. On Malik-Shāh's death he succeeded in escaping to İznik, where he was recognised as sultan. There was however a rival Turkish chief, Danişmend, whose family emerged from obscurity on the eve of the First Crusade. Its territory lay in the northern parts of central Asia Minor, with Sivas, Tokat and Amasya among its cities. During the twelfth century the power of the Danişmendids declined, and their lands were eventually absorbed into the Seljuk sultanate of Rūm.

The Armenians' original homeland, Greater Armenia, lay to the north of Lake Van in the vicinity of Mount Ararat. During the early eleventh century it was brought into the Byzantine Empire. Gagik II, the last king of Greater Armenia, was deprived of his realm and re-established in Cappadocia (eastern Anatolia), which led to an extensive Armenian migration to that region of the Empire. Armenian governors were appointed to the fortresses of the eastern Taurus and the cities that lay beyond. There had long been Armenian migration into Cilicia, where a fertile plain watered by the Tarsus Çayı (on which the city of Tarsus stands) and the rivers Seyhan and Ceyhan lies at the foot of the Taurus and the Anti-Taurus mountains to the west and north respectively. The eastern wall of Cilicia is the Amanus range. When the Byzantine defences were breached after Manzikert and the Turcomans spread over Cappadocia, there was a flood of migrants into Cilicia and further eastwards to the northern parts of Syria and Mesopotamia. The same course of events gave independence to the former Byzantine Armenian governors, the most successful of whom, Philaretus, established a principality extending from Cilicia eastwards to Edessa beyond the Euphrates. On his death in 1085 his territories fell apart. After a brief period of Seljuk rule Edessa passed to one of Philaretus's former Armenian officers named Toros. When the Crusaders established their states in Syria-Palestine, the bases were being laid for a new Armenian polity to their north, in what became known as Lesser Armenia.

chapter one

THE FIRST CRUSADE AND ITS IMPACT

The First Crusade: territorial and demographic effects

It was upon the Near East, fragmented and divided between Byzantium and Muslim powers and their respective dependants, that the impact fell of the First Crusade. Its origins and course are well known, and need only be briefly sketched here. Pope Urban II's summons to Western Christians to set forth as warriors to the East was made on 27 November 1095 at the close of the Council of Clermont. It produced an immediate and widespread response among the peoples of France, Germany and the Low Countries.

In answer to the pope's call, an expedition chiefly recruited from the poorer people under the charismatic leadership of Peter the Hermit reached Constantinople in July and August 1096, crossed the Bosphorus, and was destroyed by Seljuk forces sent from Kılıc Arslan's capital of İznik. So ended the People's Crusade. Meanwhile the armies of the Princes' Crusade were arriving under the separate commands of Hugh, count of Vermandois (a son of Henry I of France and brother to Philip I, the reigning king), and three other noblemen, who had larger and more substantial forces. They were Godfrey of Bouillon, duke of Lower Lorraine, Bohemond of Taranto (the disinherited eldest son of Robert Guiscard, the Norman duke of Apulia and Calabria), and Raymond of Saint-Gilles, count of Toulouse. Crossing from Constantinople to Asia Minor, they took İznik and defeated Kılıc Arslan at Dorylaeum (near modern Eskişehir), holding back for a time Seljuk domination in Rūm. As they advanced towards northern Syria, Baldwin of Boulogne, Godfrey's brother, acquired from Toros, its Armenian ruler, the outlying city of Edessa (Arabic, al-Ruhā'; Turkish, Urfa), beyond the Euphrates, which with its surrounding territory he constituted into an independent county in March 1098.

Meanwhile the main body of the Crusaders proceeded to Antioch, the gateway to the south, which they took in June 1098. Yağısıyan, the governor appointed by Malik-Shāh, met his death while trying to escape from the city. Bohemond, who had taken the leading part in the capture of Antioch, claimed it as the capital of his principality. The Crusaders continued their southward march, and Jerusalem, the supreme territorial object of their ambition, was taken from the Fatimids on 15 July 1099. Godfrey of Bouillon was elected as ruler with the title of *Advocatus Sancti Sepulchri*, 'Defender of the Holy Sepulchre'. When he died a year later, his brother Baldwin was summoned from Edessa, and crowned king of Jerusalem. He went out to defeat the Fatimid army near Ascalon on 12 August. The city itself however remained a Fatimid frontier-fortress until 1153. Raymond of Saint-Gilles besieged Tripoli, a former Fatimid possession but at the time autonomous. He assumed the title of count of Tripoli, but the city fell only in 1109, four years after his death.

The Crusader states as finally established formed an elongated block of territory from north to south, the two chief cities, Antioch and Jerusalem, being about 560 km apart. The widest extent was in the most northerly sector, where Edessa lay some 250 km from the sea. From the southern frontier of the principality of Antioch stretched an attenuated central sector of mainly coastal territory, approximately to the vicinity of Tyre. The most southerly sector expanded eastwards into the Judaean highlands around Jerusalem, and then ultimately beyond into Transjordan – 'Oultrejourdain' of the Crusaders.

The territory that formed the Crusader states was thus largely acquired at the expense of the Syrian branch of the Seljuks with its two capitals at Aleppo and Damascus held respectively by Riḍwān and Dokak, the sons of Tutuş. Edessa, as we have seen, had been an Armenian lordship. Jerusalem and Ascalon formed the Fatimids' last foothold in Palestine, while their former possession of Tripoli had become autonomous under a family of Shi'i judges. Even to the Seljuks however, the losses of territory to the Crusaders were marginal, particularly as the Crusaders were never masters of the great north–south route from Aleppo by way of Ḥamāh and Ḥimṣ to Damascus, although their holdings in Transjordan intercepted its continuation to the Holy Cities of Mecca and Medina, and to Egypt. The fall of Edessa to Zangī in 1144 and the failure of the Second Crusade to take Damascus in 1148 put an end to the Frankish *Drang nach Osten*, and the later Crusades were very different in their nature from the First. They sought essentially to regain lost territory or to safeguard the remaining holdings against the Muslim great power in the region. The city of Antioch, the northern bastion of Frankish territory, had no counterpart in the south. The remote hill-city of Jerusalem, isolated and ill-provided, lacked the capability to serve as a base for attack or defence. Military operations thus devolved upon the individual Crusader states.

Two of the cities that formed the capitals of the Crusader states, Antioch and Jerusalem, outranked the others. Antioch had a history going back to the third century BC, and was an urban centre of outstanding importance in the Roman Empire. It fell to the Arabs during the caliphate of ʿUmar (634–44), and was henceforward under Muslim rule until the First Crusade, apart from the years 969 to 1084, when it was again held by the Byzantines. Jerusalem first attained importance as the capital of the Hebrew monarchy under King David (1012–972 BC). It lacked the topographical advantages and strategic importance of Antioch, but these deficiencies were more than compensated by its central position in the history of Judaism, Christianity and Islam. To Jews it was the site of the Temple and the centre of the promised Holy Land. To Christians it was the scene of the crucifixion and resurrection of Christ, commemorated in the great Church of the Holy Sepulchre. To Muslims it was the setting for the *Miʿrāj*, the Prophet's night-journey and ascent to heaven, marked by the magnificent Dome of the Rock in the area of the former Temple. Until the First Crusade, Jerusalem had been under Muslim rule since its capture by the Arabs in 638 (again during the caliphate of ʿUmar), and it was a place of pilgrimage as the third Holy City of Islam.

Edessa, taken by the Arabs in 639, had thereafter usually been under Muslim rule. It was however regained by the Byzantines in 1037, and with the collapse of Byzantine power in the east after the battle of Manzikert, it passed under Armenian rule. Tripoli, the capital of the latest of the Crusader states to be fully established, had been Muslim since the Arab conquest in the seventh century. It lay in fertile coastal territory and, as noted earlier, was the port for the hinterland from Ḥimṣ to Damascus. The last of the judges who ruled it from 1070 to 1109 was Fakhr al-Mulk Ibn ʿAmmār.

The arrival of the First Crusade in Syria-Palestine and the rapid territorial conquests of the invaders came as a shock and a surprise to the indigenous peoples. Refugees fled from the massacres committed by the Crusaders, notably at Antioch and Maʿarrat al-Nuʿmān in 1098, and in the following year at the fall of Jerusalem, which thereafter remained a city from which Muslims and Jews were excluded. Other massacres followed as more towns were captured, for example Caesarea in 1101. Sometimes the approach of the Crusaders was enough in itself to stimulate a panic flight, as when the Crusaders on the march to Jerusalem found al-Ramla already abandoned by its townspeople. Not all towns were deserted or subjected to massacre. Some capitulated to the Franks, and their inhabitants were allowed to leave under safe conduct. This happened at Arsūf on the coast of Palestine in 1101, and at the city of Tripoli in 1109. With the taking of Sidon in 1110 capitulation became the usual procedure.

The refugees made their way chiefly to the towns of Muslim Syria, especially to Damascus, Aleppo, Shayzar and Ḥamāh. Relatively few went further to the towns of the Euphrates and Tigris, or to Fatimid Egypt with its Palestinian outpost at Ascalon. Rather surprisingly, the refugees do not seem to have called for a *jihād* (Holy War) to avenge their wrongs. Certainly a summons to the *jihād* was raised in Damascus as early as 1105, but its advocate was neither a refugee nor a ruler, but a Muslim scholar, Ibn al-Sulamī, preaching and teaching in the Umayyad Mosque.

There is one exceptional instance of emigration from Frankish territory, which took place in the mid-twelfth century, long after the period of conquest. Difficulties arose between some Muslim villagers in the Nablus district and their Frankish lord, Baldwin of Ibelin. A Muslim scholar named Aḥmad b. Qudāma in the village of Jammā'īl was accused by Baldwin of withdrawing agricultural labour through his Friday sermons. Ibn Qudāma thereupon decided to emigrate, and persuaded members of his family and other persons to join him on the grounds that flight from infidel territory was required by the Sharī'a. The emigration began in 1156 and went on for some 20 years. It was technically a *hijra*, a flight from infidel to Muslim territory, based on the precedent of the Prophet's flight from Mecca to Medina. Ibn Qudāma and his fellow-migrants established themselves in the Damascus suburb of al-Ṣāliḥiyya, which duly became a centre of propaganda for the *jihād*.

The towns evacuated by the Muslims became the residence of most of the Frankish settlers in the Holy Land. They found a secure and congenial social life there, which they shared with their trading partners from the Italian republics. Their adoption of oriental styles of dress and usages earned them the scorn of European visitors. These descendants of Crusaders, born in the Holy Land, came to be called *Poulains* (Latinised as *Pullani*), literally 'Colts', a distinct breed as it were from Europeans proper.

The Frankish feudal lords in the conquered territories lived off the labours of the indigenous peasantry, partly Muslim and partly Christian. To what extent this peasant population had been reduced by flight at the time of the Crusade is unknown, but it is not likely to have been significant – a peasant clings to his land. Even if the lord lived on his estate, close personal relations with the peasantry were unlikely in view of the difference of language, culture and religion existing between them. For an understanding of the condition of the peasantry at this period we are almost entirely dependent on Frankish documentation. The agrarian regime remained essentially what it had been under the preceding Muslim landowners, although the Frankish lords were linked in a feudal network that had not existed previously. Frankish rule made no great change in the status of the peasants, which was indeed not far from servitude. The most obvious sign of the change from a Muslim to a Frankish master was the extension of the poll-tax, hitherto levied only on Christians, to the Muslim peasants also. There is little evidence of change in the methods of cultivation or the crops cultivated, although the Franks were particularly interested in the production of sugar, used both in cooking and for medicinal purposes. The peasants paid fixed dues in cash or kind on their produce, as well as giving traditional 'presents', usually three times a year.

Although the status of the peasantry as a class was low, they were organised among themselves as autonomous communities. These communities were in contact with the landowner through two local officials: the scribe and the *ra'īs*. The scribe was the lord's steward and the keeper of the necessary written records. With the imposition of Frankish rule, the steward had also to act as an interpreter in dealings between the lord and the peasants. Hence he became known as the dragoman, from the Arabic *tarjumān* (*tarjama*, to translate). The *ra'īs*, Latinised as *regulus*, was a leading man, a notable of his village community, with superior status and greater freedom than the mass of the peasantry. An example of his functions is given in a treaty concluded between Baybars and the Hospitallers in 1271, which states that if there should occur any homicide or theft in the territory of al-Marqab (the Frankish Margat), there was to be an investigation, and if the culprit was not produced within 20 days, the *ru'asā'* (plural of *ra'īs*) were to detain his nearest neighbour.

The regime of the Frankish lords was thus a transitory phenomenon, accompanied by no substantial changes in the relations between proprietor and cultivator or in the condition of the peasants themselves. There is a marked contrast between the towns, the new centres of Frankish life and culture, and the countryside, following as ever its traditional regime under its Frankish masters.

Muslim views of the First Crusade

Such was the immediate impact of the First Crusade on Asia Minor and Syria-Palestine. How was it regarded by the Muslims of the region?

The irruption of the Franks, in Arabic *al-Ifranj*, to use the Muslim term for Western Europeans in general and the Crusaders specifically, is described by the contemporary Damascene chronicler, Ibn al-Qalānisī

(d. 1160) in his account of the events of the year 490/1096–7 in these words:

> In this year there began to arrive a succession of reports that the armies of the Franks had appeared from the direction of the sea of Constantinople with forces not to be reckoned for multitude. As these reports followed one upon the other, and spread from mouth to mouth far and wide, the people grew anxious and disturbed in mind.

He goes on to describe the Crusaders' conflict with Kılıc Arslan and his rout, i.e. the battle of Dorylaeum, saying: 'When the news was received of this shameful calamity to the cause of Islām, the anxiety of the people became acute and their fear and alarm increased'.

He describes the operations against Antioch and its fall in these words:

> The lords of the pedigree steeds were put to flight, and the sword was unsheathed on the footsoldiers who had volunteered for the cause of God, who had girt themselves for the Holy War, and were vehement in their desire to strike a blow for the Faith and for the protection of the Muslims.[1]

He then traces the southward advance of the Crusaders, culminating in an unemotional account of the taking of Jerusalem, followed by the victory over the Fatimid forces outside Ascalon. On the whole Ibn al-Qalānisī shows more concern over the loss of Muslim lives than over the capture of Antioch or even the fall of the Holy City of Jerusalem.

A more emotional view of events, stimulated by strong religious feeling, is presented by another contemporary Arabic writer, the Islamic propagandist Ibn al-Sulamī. In 1105 he produced in Damascus his book *Kitāb al-jihād*, 'The book of the Holy War', in which he ascribes the successes of the Franks to the irreligion and disunity of the Muslims. He was in his time a voice crying in the wilderness, as the Muslim powers of the Syrian hinterland showed little concern over the irruption of the Frankish barbarians into the maritime fringe of the region. It is interesting that Ibn al-Sulamī does not see the Crusade and the consequent losses of Muslim territory in isolation, but views them as part of a wider Frankish assault upon Islam as witnessed by the conquest of Sicily and of many towns in Spain.

More generally the Crusades, and even the conquest and settlement of Syria-Palestine by the Franks, were not treated by the Arabic chroniclers as a distinct category of historical events. There were reports of particular episodes dispersed in city chronicles, dynastic histories and works of wider scope, giving the impression of the relative marginality of these events to the history of the Islamic Near East. For example, H. A. R. Gibb's book, the source of the above excerpts, entitled *The*

Damascus Chronicle of the Crusades, is translated from Ibn al-Qalānisī's *Dhayl ta'rīkh Dimashq*, i.e. 'The continuation of the chronicle of Damascus'. It seems that the first conspectus of the Crusades as such by an Arabic writer did not appear until 1520, when a certain Aḥmad al-Ḥarīrī completed a work entitled *al-I'lām wa'l-tabyīn fī khurūj al-Firanj al-malā'īn 'alā diyār al-Muslimīn*, 'Information and exposition of the irruption of the accursed Franks upon the Muslim homelands'.

The wider historical significance of the First Crusade, foreshadowed by Ibn al-Sulamī, was developed about a century later by one of the greatest of the Arabic chroniclers, Ibn al-Athīr (1160–1233) in his monumental universal history entitled *al-Kāmil fi'l-ta'rīkh*, 'The Complete History'. His account of the origins of the First Crusade is of interest as showing the outlook and limitations of a well-educated and highly competent Muslim chronicler.

Describing the events of 491/1097–8, Ibn al-Athīr gives an account of the capture of Antioch by the Franks, which he prefaces as follows:

> The first appearance of the Franks and the increase of their authority, their setting out for the land of Islam and their capture of a part of it, were in the year 478/1085–86, when they took Toledo and other cities of the land of Andalusia as mentioned previously. Then in the year 484/1091–92 they proceeded to the island of Sicily as I have also mentioned. They penetrated also into the borders of Ifrīqiya [Africa]. They took some of it, which was retaken; then they made other conquests as you may see.
>
> In the year 490/1096–97 they set out for the land of Syria. The reason for their invasion was that their king, Baldwin, assembled a great host of Franks. He was a kinsman by marriage of Roger the Frank who ruled Sicily. He sent an envoy to Roger saying to him, 'I have assembled a great host and am coming to you, and proceeding from you to conquer Ifrīqiya; and I shall be your neighbour'.

This news was unwelcome to Roger, who regarded with dismay the prospect of having to supply Baldwin with money, ships and troops. Furthermore Baldwin's proposed operations would damage his good relations with the ruler of Tunis.

> He [Roger] summoned the envoy, and said to him, 'If you are determined to fight a Holy War against the Muslims, the best thing would be to conquer Jerusalem. You will liberate it from their hands, and the glory will be yours. As for Ifrīqiya, there are sworn treaties between ourselves and its people'.
>
> So they made their preparations and set out for Syria.

Ibn al-Athīr presents an interesting view of the origins of the First Crusade. Although he describes the expedition to Jerusalem as a *jihād*, the pope plays no part in its initiation or organisation; it results from a deal in realpolitik between two Christian rulers. Presumably Baldwin is described as king of the Franks and leader of the Crusade because he became eventually the first king of Jerusalem. Since he was followed in due course by four other Baldwins, the name may have seemed almost like a regal or dynastic title to the Arabic chronicler. Roger of Sicily is presented as a devious and subtle politician. He diverts Baldwin from attempting the conquest of Ifrīqiya, here signifying Tunisia, fearing the loss of tribute paid by the Zirid ruler, Tamīm b. al-Muʿizz (1062–1108), while tacitly hoping to conquer the country himself when the time should be right.

It is important to bear in mind that the Arabic presentation of the Crusades was the work of Muslim chroniclers who had been formed by a traditional education in the Islamic religious sciences, designed to produce scholars in theology, the Sharīʿa and the Arabic language. Their experience lay primarily in the administration of the law and the state, and they were skilled in court politics and in handling rulers. They viewed and presented events within a dogmatic framework from the standpoint of pious, cultured and experienced Muslims. *Mutatis mutandis* the same was true of their Western counterparts, formed by a traditional Christian religious education, who also viewed the events transacted in Syria-Palestine from the standpoint of a dogmatic faith, and gave them an ideological presentation in their chronicles.

The impact of the First Crusade on the Byzantine Empire

The impact of the First Crusade on the Byzantine Empire and the Armenians of Cilicia, northern Syria and northern Mesopotamia, the Christian neighbours of the Crusader states, must now be considered.

The Byzantine Empire had been involved in the crusading venture from the start. To judge from the earliest account of Urban II's summons to the Crusade, written by Fulcher of Chartres, a cleric who was probably present at the Council of Clermont, the pope's call was made specifically in response to an appeal sent by the Emperor Alexius I Comnenus. At the preceding Council of Piacenza in March 1095, the emperor's envoys had asked for warriors from the West, who would aid him against the conquering Seljuks, and thereby defend Christendom. Some mention was perhaps made to Turkish rule in Jerusalem as a religious and emotional bait. What the emperor hoped for was clearly the recruitment of mercenaries to serve in the imperial forces. On such recruits from many peoples, Normans, English and Turks among them, the military strength of Byzantium depended at this period. A few years earlier, Robert, count of Flanders, when returning from pilgrimage, met

Alexius and bound himself by oath to send an armed contingent of 500 men to serve the emperor. Such, presumably, but on a much greater scale, was what Alexius hoped would be the response to his appeal.

This, according to Fulcher of Chartres, was faithfully transmitted by the pope to his audience at Clermont. He is represented as saying:

> Hastening to the way, you must help your brothers living in the Orient, who need your aid, for which they have already cried out many times. For, as most of you have been told, the Turks . . . who have penetrated within the borders of Romania [i.e. Anatolia] even to the Mediterranean to that point which they call the Arm of Saint George [i.e. the Bosphorus], in occupying more and more of the lands of the Christians, have overcome them, already victims of seven battles, and have killed and captured them, have overthrown churches and laid waste God's kingdom. If you permit this supinely for very long, God's faithful ones will be still further subjected.[2]

There is no reference here to Jerusalem as the goal of the Crusade, while on the other hand the pope dwells on the damage done to the Byzantine Empire. Admittedly, however, references to the liberation of Jerusalem appear prominently in other early accounts of Urban's appeal.

Alexius's request for aid had come at a critical time in the relations between the Orthodox and Catholic Churches. Half a century earlier disagreements between the two great branches of Christianity, which had been growing for a long period, developed into open schism in 1054, when the papal legate in Constantinople laid a bull of excommunication directed against the Orthodox patriarch on the high altar of Saint Sophia, and the patriarch in turn excommunicated the legate. Times and ecclesiastical leaders had changed, and the Emperor Alexius was not dominated by the patriarch of his day as his predecessor had been 50 years before. In 1089 Urban wrote to him, taking the first step towards restoring good relations between the Churches, although the doctrinal and liturgical schism was not healed then or later.

The emperor hoped, as mentioned, to obtain a force of mercenaries from the West. Instead, a vast horde of armed pilgrims on their way to Jerusalem converged on his capital, creating enormous problems of security, provisioning and logistics for the Byzantine authorities. Among the nobles who brought contingents of Crusaders, one particularly ill-omened in Byzantine eyes was Bohemond of Taranto, the eldest son of Robert Guiscard. His father was the most successful of several brothers from Normandy who played a leading part in the warfare and politics of southern Italy in the second half of the eleventh century. In 1059 Pope Nicholas II had invested Robert as his vassal with the dukedom of Apulia and Calabria, also prospectively with Sicily, although the actual conquest of the island from the Muslims was to be achieved by his brother Roger (d. 1101). Byzantine sovereignty and administration lingered in southern Italy after the loss of all other possessions in the western Mediterranean, only to be finally extinguished in 1071 (the year of Manzikert), when Robert Guiscard took Bari, the Byzantine headquarters in Apulia. There were however already tentative moves towards a mutual understanding. The Emperor Romanus Diogenes proposed a marriage alliance which was rejected by Robert, but after Manzikert fresh proposals were put forward by the Emperor Michael VII, and in 1074 Robert sent his daughter, appropriately renamed Helena, for betrothal to the emperor's son. Michael was deposed in 1078, and thereafter Robert seems to have aimed at more direct control of Byzantine policy. He produced a pseudo-Michael, and in 1081 led an expedition in his name to Dyrrachium (medieval Durazzo, now Dürres) on the Adriatic coast. He was accompanied by Bohemond, whose mother he had repudiated, and who thereby found himself deprived of his inheritance. They took Dyrrachium in 1082, and Robert returned to Italy. Bohemond, in search of territorial compensation for his loss, pressed on with the invasion. He was defeated by Alexius in 1083 and went back to Italy, while the territory he had conquered in the Balkans was reintegrated into the Empire.

When Bohemond and the other noble Crusaders arrived at Constantinople in 1097, the emperor endeavoured to secure his authority over them and his rights to any prospective conquests by requiring an oath of fealty. This was given with greater or less reluctance by the nobles, and by Raymond of Saint-Gilles in a modified form. Bohemond, anxious to regain credit with Alexius, swore that he would neither withhold any former imperial possessions nor allow others to do so.

When the nobles' contingents first crossed over to Asia Minor, they fulfilled their sworn obligations to the emperor. On 14 May 1097 siege was laid to İznik, at that time the capital of the Sultan Kılıc Arslan. He himself was absent, but returned to face defeat outside the city. Aided by a naval squadron supplied by the emperor, the blockade brought about the capitulation of the Turkish garrison on 19 June. It surrendered to the emperor, not to the Crusaders, who were thus disappointed in their hopes of sacking the city, and annoyed by the safe evacuation of Kılıc Arslan's family and nobles to Constantinople. The resentment and suspicion that had developed since the first arrival of the Crusaders were increasingly voiced. The anonymous Norman knight in Bohemond's contingent who produced the earliest Western account of the Crusade stigmatises the emperor's action as that of 'a fool as well as a knave', and accuses him of sparing the Turks 'so that he could have them to injure the Franks and obstruct their crusade'.[3]

Nevertheless the appearance of harmony was maintained during the next stage of the Crusade – the advance across Anatolia to Antioch. Bohemond and his Norman–Italian contingent were accompanied on the march by a Byzantine general of Turkish origin named Taticius, with a detachment of troops to guide the Crusaders through this unknown country. The advance began on 26 June 1097, and four days later the Crusaders encountered and routed the forces of Kılıc Arslan at Dorylaeum. Although the Crusaders passed through or by several inportant cities such as Iconium (modern Konya), Heraclea (Ereğli), where they defeated a Turkish force, and Caesarea (Kayseri), no attempt was made to effect a permanent conquest, and at the same time there was no thought of returning these former Byzantine possessions to the emperor.

The problem however arose acutely when the long siege of Antioch (from 21 October 1097 to 3 June 1098) ended, and the Crusaders' victory was sealed by the defeat on 28 June by the defeat of a relieving force led by Kırboğa, the ruler of Mosul. Early in February while the siege was proceeding, Taticius (whose advice had been disregarded as usual) left the camp, and returned to the Emperor. He is mentioned by the Norman knight for the first time on this occasion, and described as 'our enemy' who 'is a liar and always will be'. At this juncture Alexius had a field army at Philomelium (modern Akşehir), but was deterred from action by the arrival of Stephen of Blois, who had left the siege with deserters before it ended, and reported that the Crusaders were threatened by Kırboğa. With Antioch thus apparently in a hopeless situation, the emperor gave up the project of going to the relief of his allies, and returned to Constantinople.

This left the way clear for Bohemond. It was he who had been in touch with the renegade Fīrūz who enabled the Crusaders to enter the city, and, when it fell, Bohemond's flag flew over it. When Kırboğa too was defeated and the citadel surrendered, Bohemond advanced a claim to the city. Alexius had no representative present to demand that the city should be handed over in accordance with the agreement made with the leading Crusaders. So although Bohemond's claim was contested by Raymond of Saint-Gilles, it was generally accepted, and thereby the foundations of the principality of Antioch were laid by its first prince. There was also no proposal to return Edessa to the Byzantines. Although its ruler Toros might have a shadow of Byzantine legitimacy as a former retainer of Philaretus, this did not survive his passing, when Edessa became the capital of the Frankish county ruled by Baldwin of Boulogne.

The status of Antioch had thus been decided by events, but the question of relations with the emperor remained, since the Crusaders' agreement with him extended to all the former Byzantine possessions. In July 1098 Hugh of Vermandois went as the Crusaders' envoy to ask Alexius to come to Antioch. The emperor did not respond until the spring of 1099, when he sent envoys to Bohemond demanding the surrender of Antioch. The demand was rejected. In the meantime, on 13 January 1099, after pressure from the rank and file, who were anxious to complete their pilgrimage, a crusading force marched out under the command of Raymond of Saint-Gilles. His first operation was to besiege 'Arqa, lying north-east of Tripoli. There he was met in April by the emperor's envoys, who again demanded the restoration of Antioch to the Empire. They were again refused on the grounds that Alexius himself had broken the agreement by failing to provide the Crusaders with supplies and to follow them up with an army. The envoys promised that Alexius would come bringing gifts by 25 June. Raymond, once a strong opponent of the emperor, now headed a faction prepared to abide by the agreement and await the coming of Alexius. Bohemond naturally took a different position. To him the withdrawal of the emperor from Philomelium and the abandonment by Taticius of the Crusaders at Antioch were breaches of the agreement. Others thought that Alexius's much delayed response to the urgings of Hugh of Vermandois rendered the agreement invalid. The rejectionists triumphed; the march to Jerusalem was resumed, and the Byzantine envoys left empty-handed. There was no question of the surrender of Jerusalem to Byzantine rule, although Raymond, still faithful to his agreement, negotiated with Alexius in due course his prospective tenure of Tripoli.

The impact of the First Crusade on the Armenians

In the south-eastern part of the former borderlands of the Byzantine Empire before Manzikert lay the coastal territory of Cilicia, shut in by the three ranges of the Taurus, Anti-Taurus and Amanus Mountains. Commencing as a narrow strip by the ancient port of Seleucia (now Silifke), it broadened out into the Cilician Plain. The entrance from central Anatolia was the Cilician Gates (Gülek Boğazı), a narrow and strategically important pass by the upper stream of the Tarsus Çayı. Turning south and again reduced to a narrow strip, Cilicia ended on the eastern coast of the Gulf of İskenderun.

This region had long received immigrants and settlers from Greater Armenia, the original homeland, which lay around Mount Ararat between Lake Van and the Caucasus. The final incorporation of Greater Armenia in the Byzantine Empire in 1045, and Turcoman invasions and conquests after Manzikert, produced two further waves of immigration into Cilicia. Meanwhile the Armenians had spread far to the east of Cilicia, into the hill country in the north of Syria and Mesopotamia. Some Armenians took service under the Byzantines, and were appointed governors or military officers in Cilicia and these more easterly lands. When Byzantine power collapsed in the east, they took the opportunity to establish themselves as warlords. At the outset the most successful of them was a former general of Romanus IV Diogenes named Philaretus, who between 1078 and his death in 1085 built up a principality extending from Cilicia to Edessa.

After the death of Philaretus domination over the cities and their surrounding territories was seized by a number of warlords, some of whom had served under the Byzantine emperor, and had consequently accepted the Greek Orthodox faith in place of their traditional Armenian confession. At the time of the coming of the Crusaders, there were six important Armenian principalities. Two key fortresses at the southern end of the Cilician Gates, Lampron (now Namrun) and Babaron (Candır Kale) were granted by the Byzantine Armenian governor of Tarsus to his general Oshin, the founder of the historically significant Hetoumid clan. Further to the north-east but still within Cilicia proper lay the principality of Constantine, the head of the rival Roupenid clan, and, unlike Oshin, faithful to the Armenian Church. His power was based upon the two fortresses of Partzapert, held by his grandfather, and Vahka (now Feke). Both of these lay north of Sis, the future capital of the kingdom of Lesser Armenia. Outside the geographical limits of Cilicia and somewhat to the north-east lay the principality of Maraş, centred on the city now named Kahramanmaraş. Its ruler at the time of the First Crusade was Tatoul, formerly a Byzantine official, a member of the Greek Orthodox Church. The fortresses of Raban (now Altınaşkale) and Kesoun, lying east of Maraş towards the upper Euphrates, were held under Seljuk overlordship by Kogh Vasil, Armenian by nationality and religion. To their north and again in the vicinity of the upper Euphrates was the principality of Malatya, held under Seljuk suzerainty by Gabriel, formerly one of Philaretus's officers and Greek Orthodox by faith. Finally beyond lay Edessa (modern Turkish, Şanlıurfa), where the warlord was Toros, another of Philaretus's Greek Orthodox officers, who had received from Alexius Comnenus the Byzantine title of *curopalates.* He was the son-in-law of Gabriel of Malatya.

In contrast to the suspicious attitude of the Byzantines towards the Crusaders and the animosity that developed between the two parties, the Armenians welcomed the coming of the Franks, and mutual relations were generally both close and friendly. The fact that the leaders on both sides belonged to an equestrian warrior aristocracy (as was also true of the Turks), and that the Armenian social system could be assimilated to Western feudalism, may have had some part in this. An early example of their good relationship occurred during the siege of İznik, when Baldwin of Boulogne took into his entourage Kogh Vasil's brother Bagrat, who had served in the Byzantine army. This may have been a factor in the highly significant decision taken by Baldwin and Tancred, Bohemond's nephew, at Heraclea (Ereğli) to separate their forces from the main army and make their way through the Cilician Gates into Cilicia itself, advancing on Antioch by this southerly route. The other leaders decided to take a longer route eastwards, and descend on Antioch from the north. Their choice seems to have been made on the advice of Taticius, who was perhaps following a Byzantine policy to regain control of this region.

Having entered Cilicia and taken Tarsus, Baldwin and Tancred parted company. Helped by Oshin of Lampron, Tancred took Adana and Alexandretta (now İskenderun), and then joined the other Crusaders at the siege of Antioch, while Baldwin took Mamistra (now Yakapınar) and proceeded to Edessa. There, as has been mentioned, he was welcomed by Toros, whom he succeeded as lord of Edessa. In the meantime the main Crusader army, in the words of the Norman knight, 'entered the land of the Armenians, thirsting and craving for the blood of the Turks'. From Heraclea it advanced northwards to Augustopolis (not far from modern Turkish Niğde), which it gave to an Armenian ally named Simeon to defend against the Turks. The army continued its northward march to Caesarea, and then turned south-eastwards, receiving on the way the surrender of Comana and Coxon (Turkish, Göksun) at the hands of their Armenian inhabitants. After a difficult mountain crossing it descended on Maraş. There it was welcomed by Tatoul, whom Taticius confirmed in office, and thence pressed on to Antioch.

The good understanding between the Armenian warlords and the Frankish leaders was underpinned in the next few years by interconfessional marriages. Baldwin of Boulogne's wife had died at Maraş in 1097, and after he became count of Edessa he married Arda, a granddaughter of the Roupenid chief Constantine. Baldwin of Le Bourg, who was to succeed Baldwin of Boulogne as count of Edessa and king of Jerusalem in turn, married Morfia, a daughter of Gabriel of Malatya. Through their eldest daughter, Melisende, a Frankish–Armenian dynasty was established on the throne of Jerusalem, when her husband, Count Fulk of Anjou, became king of Jerusalem in right of his wife. Meanwhile Joscelin of Courtenay, who had succeeded Baldwin of Le Bourg, his kinsman and former lord, as count of Edessa in 1119, was married to a daughter of Constantine.

It is clear from what has been said that the Franks of the Crusader states had little difficulty in establishing a close relationship both physically and culturally with the Armenians of Cilicia and neighbouring territories. The affinity of the Armenians with the Franks and Western Christendom was dramatically exhibited on 6 January 1198, when Leon II, the Roupenid ruler of Cilicia, was crowned king of Lesser Armenia. The crown was sent by the Holy Roman Emperor Henry VI, the son and successor of the Crusader Frederick Barbarossa.

Technical and cultural interchange

As the Crusader states were essentially an alien and hostile implant into the Islamic society of the Near East, it is hardly surprising that evidence of technical and cultural interchange is very meagre. It is in the sphere of military developments that such interchange is clearest.

Both the Frankish and the Muslim powers depended on their castles to dominate and demarcate the lands that they held, and siege warfare to capture or destroy strongholds was a more frequent military activity than the waging of pitched battles. In consequence both sides made frequent use of machinery drawn up for use in their siege-trains. At first, Frankish siege-engines were used primarily for offensive operations, and their superiority was secured by better skill in carpentry and in the organisation of transport. Muslim siege equipment was in this phase more lightly constructed and was used for defensive purposes. The siege of Montferrand (i.e. Baʿrīn, to the north-west of Ḥimṣ) seems to mark a turning point, since this was the occasion for the first use by the Muslims of heavy siege equipment. Moreover it was successful; the stronghold fell to the Muslims and was never regained by the Franks. As Frankish confidence in the security of their fortresses diminished, they responded by adopting a new form of defence in the construction of concentric castles with two or three lines of walls. From the 1160s onwards castles of this type were built or existing ones modified. Such construction was an expensive business, and so castles passed from private ownership into the possession of the wealthy military orders. The growing effectiveness of the Muslims in this aspect of warfare is linked with the unification of their territories and political power by the Zangids and Ayyubids.

In medieval Spain the transmission of learning from Muslims to Christians, notably aided by Jewish intermediaries, was an important consequence of the juxtaposition of the communities. Evidence for similar developments in the Frankish states seems to be almost entirely lacking. An exception should be made of Antioch, a city of very mixed population, which before the Crusades had stood on the frontier of Christendom and Islam. The Pisans were given a quarter in Antioch by Tancred in 1108 in remuneration for the assistance furnished to the Crusaders by their ships. In consequence a channel was created whereby Arabic manuscripts were transmitted from Antioch to Pisa, which became a centre for translating activities. In the early twelfth century a translator known as Stephen of Pisa produced a Latin version of an important medical treatise. This was the *Kitāb al-malakī* of ʿAlī b. al-ʿAbbās al-Majūsī (known in the West as Haly Abbas), which was composed in the mid-tenth century.

In the Frankish states recourse was frequently made to Christian, Jewish and Muslim physicians. The family of Abū Sulaymān Dāwūd, who was by origin a Christian of Jerusalem, produced several doctors. Abū Sulaymān himself was working in Egypt at the end of the Fatimid period, but in 1167 he was taken with his five sons to Jerusalem by King Amalric, to treat his leprous son, later King Baldwin IV. The family were still there in 1184, when one of Abū Sulaymān's sons (who had perhaps better access to sources of intelligence than the Frankish government) predicted the fall of Jerusalem to Saladin. When this duly occurred, the family entered the service of the Ayyubids. It has been estimated that a third of the doctors in Syria and two-thirds of those in Egypt were Christians, Jews or Samaritans.

A root cause of the misunderstanding between the Frankish states and their Muslim neighbours was the linguistic obstacle. The Crusaders and their successors in the Frankish states show little sign of having acquired a knowledge of Arabic. No doubt a lingua franca arose between the Franks and their Arabic-speaking servants. In the management of agrarian affairs for Frankish landowners, the scribe assumed the functions of an interpreter. A few Frankish notables are mentioned in Western sources as knowing Arabic. Outstanding among them is William of Tyre. He was born in Jerusalem about 1130, and studied at Paris and Bologna, and also visited Rome and Constantinople. His great chronicle of the kingdom of Jerusalem, *Historia rerum in partibus transmarinis gestarum*, extends from 1095 to 1184, shortly before his death and three years before Saladin's victory in the battle of Ḥaṭṭīn. He also wrote a history of the oriental rulers which is unfortunately (and significantly) lost, although the substance of some parts is indicated in his surviving chronicle. But even William of Tyre's knowledge of literary Arabic has been impugned, so that here as elsewhere it appears that the cultural links between the Franks and their neighbours were of a very tenuous character.

Notes

1. H. A. R. Gibb (tr.), *The Damascus Chronicle of the Crusades*, London: Luzac & Co., 1967 (hereafter Gibb, *Damascus Chronicle*), pp. 41, 42, 46.
2. Edward Peters (ed.), *The First Crusade*, Philadelphia: University of Pennsylvania Press, 1971 (hereafter Peters, *First Crusade*), p. 30.
3. Rosalind Hill (tr. and ed.), *Gesta Francorum*, London: Thomas Nelson & Son, 1962, p. 17.

chapter two

POLITICS AND WARFARE: 1097–1119

The settlement of the Crusaders in Syria-Palestine and the consequent establishment of the Frankish states was resisted both by forces organised by individual local rulers and by armies sent under generals commissioned by the Seljuk sultan. Byzantium, which had a legitimate claim to Antioch, regarded Bohemond I and his successors as usurpers, so they had to reckon also with danger from this side. This chapter will deal separately with these two threats to Antioch, and then turn to the formation of the kingdom of Jerusalem.

Antioch and its Muslim neighbours: 1100–19

The most serious threat to the Franks of Antioch came from Riḍwān, the elder son of Tutuş and his successor as lord of Aleppo. In June 1100 Riḍwān marched westwards from Aleppo to expel the Franks from Kallā in the borderland between his lordship and Antioch. There he was met and routed by a Frankish force assembled from the neighbouring towns and commanded by Bohemond. In consequence the Franks were able to add a strip of territory to their holdings, and they made preparations to besiege Aleppo itself. The plan was given up after a day or two, when news came of the siege of Malatya to the far north of Antiochene territory by the Turkish Emir Danişmend. In an attempt to relieve Malatya Bohemond was captured and held until 1103.

The next major clash occurred in May 1104, when a Frankish army commanded by Bohemond and Baldwin of Le Bourg, the count of Edessa and future King Baldwin II of Jerusalem, endeavoured to take the city of Ḥarrān lying south of Edessa on the Balīkh, a tributary of the Euphrates. This was an important key city between Aleppo and Mosul. A relieving force under the command of Çökürmiş, the governor of Mosul, and Sökmen, the Artukid lord of Ḥiṣn Kayfā, inflicted a heavy defeat on the Franks. Bohemond succeeded in escaping to Edessa, but

Baldwin was captured together with Joscelin of Courtenay, the lord of Turbessel (Arabic, Tall Bāshir), who was to succeed him in due course as count of Edessa. For Antioch, this meant that Riḍwān was able to retake all but one of the borderland towns that had been the Frankish bases for attacks on Aleppo.

Shortly afterwards Bohemond left for Italy, whence he planned to attack the Byzantine Empire in Europe. He was defeated by Alexius I Comnenus in 1108, and died in 1111. He was succeeded as ruler of Antioch by his nephew, Tancred of Hauteville, who had been his regent while Bohemond was Danişmend's captive. In April 1105 Tancred succeeded in redressing the balance of power between Antioch and Aleppo. Armenians in the fortress town of Artāḥ, in the northern borders of Antioch, surrendered it to Riḍwān because of Frankish oppression. Tancred led a relieving expedition from Antioch, as did Riḍwān with all his forces from Aleppo. In the ensuing clash the Muslim infantry stood firm but the cavalry was broken, and the remnants of the army fled from the field. The Frankish cavalry followed up its victory and hunted down the military and civilian fugitives. This, says the Muslim chronicler, was a worse disaster than Kallā, and Riḍwān found himself hemmed in on all his borders. He had no further major clashes with the Franks, and died in August 1113. His brother, Dokak of Damascus, had already died in June 1104, leaving a son, a minor, who died soon afterwards. Thenceforward, as indeed had previously been the case, the *Atabeg* Tuğtigin was the effective ruler of Damascus and the strong man of the region.

During the years following Tancred's victory at Artāḥ there were signs that the nominal overlord of the region, the Seljuk sultan, was beginning to take a direct interest in the Frankish presence, unlike the negligence that Ibn al-Sulamī had reprehended in the earlier years of the twelfth century. Ibn al-Sulamī's lectures and writings may have been a stimulus to the rulers; of greater significance probably were the more settled relations among the members of the Seljuk clan after the troubles following the death of Malik-Shāh in 1092. Tutuş, as we have seen, participated in the succession struggles to his own destruction, and the ultimate victor was Malik-Shāh's eldest son, Berkyaruk, whose supremacy was contested however by his half-brothers, Muḥammad Tapar and Aḥmad Sencer, until his death in 1105. Thereupon Tapar made Sencer his deputy over the eastern provinces of the Seljuk Empire, while he himself retained the rule over the west. Meanwhile the Seljuks of Rūm were developing their power independently in Anatolia, while the sons and successors of Tutuş ruled from Damascus and Aleppo.

It is significant that when Tapar went to Baghdad for his formal investiture as sultan by the Caliph al-Mustaẓhir (1094–1118), he was accompanied by Çökürmiş, the powerful lord of Mosul. It is significant also that henceforward warfare against the Frankish states, initiated or sponsored by the sultan, was launched under the command of the current lord of Mosul. Over some 20 years these virtually autonomous governors underwent a number of changes. Çökürmiş was overthrown by a successor named Çavli, sent by Sultan Tapar in 1106. Failing to satisfy the sultan by not sending him a share of the booty he had acquired, he was replaced in the middle of 1108 by the Amir Mawdūd b. Altıntigin, a successful military commander. Inspired by the sultan to take serious action against the Franks, Mawdūd, in alliance with the powerful *atabeg* of Damascus, Tuğtigin, carried out two indecisive campaigns in 1110 and 1111. A further campaign was fought in 1113 against Baldwin I near the Sea of Galilee, and the king was defeated. Unable to hold the territory that he had gained, Mawdūd was compelled to fall back to Damascus, where he was murdered in October of the same year.

Following the death of Mawdūd, Sultan Tapar appointed the Amir Aksungur al-Bursuqī to govern Mosul, nominally as the *atabeg* of one of his young sons. Like Mawdūd before him, Aksungur was commissioned to carry on warfare against the Franks. İlgazi, the Artukid lord of Mardin, gave him reluctant military support, and in 1114 their combined armies attacked Edessa. The capital held out, but the county was ravaged by the invaders. A clash between the two Muslim leaders then ensued, and Aksungur was defeated by İlgazi's Turcomans.

Thereupon Aksungur was dismissed from his command, and in May 1115 the sultan committed the army of Mosul and the duty of *jihād* against the Franks to a man from the East, Porsuk (a Turkish name Arabicised as Bursuq), who was a Turk and the governor of the Persian city of Hamadhān. Porsuk's first act was to march on Aleppo, which had fallen into anarchy after the death of Riḍwān. On receiving Porsuk's demand for the surrender of the city, the regent called on İlgazi and Tuğtigin for help. They joined him in Aleppo. Porsuk withdrew, and the Muslim chiefs went on to ask Roger of Salerno, the ruler of Antioch, for his assistance. He duly responded. The Frankish force took Porsuk by surprise, and defeated him at Tall Dānith in the Antioch–Aleppo borderland. This Frankish–Muslim coalition against an outsider was a phenomenon repeated in later phases of the relationships between the Crusader states and their neighbours, and was to become a feature of policy as the *lā maqām* doctrine, i.e. that the Syrian states would form a coalition against an intruder out of fear there would be no place (Arabic, *lā maqām*) for them under a new political regime.

Developments in Syria now reverted to the play of local politics. Tuğtigin had his status as ruler of Damascus officially confirmed by the sultan in 1116. Aleppo invited İlgazi to take the city over at the end of 1118. This he did, and installed his son as regent. A principal cause of the invitation was the growing pressure from Roger of Salerno, who was increasing the Frankish territorial holdings around Aleppo. Roger responded to the change of masters in Aleppo in December 1118 by taking the town of ʿAzāz, lying to the north of Aleppo on the route from Antioch to Edessa. İlgazi thereupon prepared his forces, which were largely made up of Turcomans, for an attack on Antioch in the cause of the *jihād*, and allied with Tuğtigin to obtain the support of Damascus. The Damascene troops however failed to arrive, and İlgazi went on to encounter the Franks not far from Artāḥ on 28 June 1119. The battle went down in Frankish history as *Ager Sanguinis*, the Field of Blood. The Franks were overcome, and Roger of Salerno himself was killed in the fighting. The principality of Antioch lost its main border settlements, and King Baldwin II assumed the direction of its affairs as regent for Bohemond I's infant son, Bohemond II, then in Italy.

Antioch and Byzantium to 1119

Bohemond of Taranto, the founder and first ruler of the principality of Antioch, was a talented and ruthless opportunist. The disinherited son of Robert Guiscard, he was ready to take any chance that offered to enhance his status and power when on Crusade. He was one of the first leaders to give the oath of fealty to Alexius Comnenus, and hoped to become the leader of the Crusade in the emperor's service. Disappointed in this, he saw in Antioch a means to realise his ambitions. During the siege it was he who conspired with Fīrūz for the betrayal of the city, and when Antioch was taken it was left in Bohemond's hands pending the emperor's arrival. But in spite of negotiations at ʿArqa between the leading Crusaders and Byzantine envoys, the emperor never did come; and Bohemond contended that Alexius's withdrawal from Philomelium invalidated his claim to Antioch. In 1100 he was duly invested as prince of Antioch by the papal legate, Archbishop Daimbert of Pisa.

So was established the independent principality of Antioch. It was in some respects isolated among the Crusader states. Between Bohemond and his nearest neighbour, Baldwin of Edessa, there were no ties of blood. Bohemond and his successors until the death of Roger of Salerno on the Field of Blood in 1119 were Normans. Baldwin was a Lorrainer, and was soon to succeed his brother Godfrey, and become king of Jerusalem. Antioch was the only Frankish capital directly threatened by the Byzantines. Any territorial expansion of the principality meant either a conflict with Muslim neighbours in the east, especially Aleppo, or hostilities or an uneasy peace with the Byzantines or Armenian warlords in the north. This set the pattern of diplomatic and military relations for many years. A more immediate danger to Antioch was the coastal enclave and port of Latakia, which was held by a Byzantine garrison from Cyprus.

In spite of his ambition Bohemond achieved nothing against Byzantium in either sector of their confrontation. Lacking maritime power, he could not act effectively against Latakia until he joined forces with a Genoese fleet under Daimbert of Pisa. Their joint siege of Latakia was ended on the arrival of a Crusader army from the south, commanded by Raymond of Saint-Gilles and Robert of Normandy on their way home after the taking of Jerusalem. Hostilities between Bohemond and Raymond, rivals of old, were averted through the archbishop of Pisa's mediation, and Latakia was occupied by Raymond's forces, probably by agreement with the Byzantines.

Then after visiting Jerusalem with Baldwin of Edessa, Bohemond led a force to the north to attack Maraş, which formed a Byzantine base under an Armenian governor. He was however persuaded by another Armenian, the governor of Malatya, to come to his relief, and this led to Bohemond's capture by the Emir Danişmend, as already mentioned. His nephew, Tancred of Hauteville, as regent in his absence, won a transient success by establishing control over Maraş and Cilicia generally in 1101. He renewed the blockade of Latakia, which surrendered early in 1103. When Bohemond returned from captivity, the battle on the Balīkh was as fatal to the principality's hold on the north as to its position in the borderlands with Aleppo. Revolts against the Franks by the Armenians of Cilicia ensued, enabling the Byzantines to regain their overlordship of the region. At the same time a Byzantine fleet recaptured the harbour and town of Latakia, although not the citadel. Hemmed in on every side, Bohemond departed for Europe to gather fresh forces and to launch a direct assault there on the Byzantine Empire.

The second regency of Tancred of Hauteville followed in Antioch. It opened with the victory of Artāḥ and the rapid revival of the principality. An attempt was made to regain control of Cilicia. This began with a northern campaign, perhaps in 1107, when the Emperor Alexius recalled his commander in Tarsus to assist in the resistance to Bohemond in Europe. By 1111 a Crusader held the title of 'prince of the towns of Tarsus and Mamistra' (i.e. Misis), implying Tancred's effective overlordship of Cilicia. The recall of the Byzantine commander from Latakia, which was also necessitated by the operations against Bohemond, enabled Tancred to regain the town in 1108.

Alexius had meanwhile stopped Bohemond at Dyrrachium, and negotiations between the two culminated in the Treaty of Devol in 1108, by which Bohemond declared himself to be the emperor's vassal, and undertook (among other ineffective promises) to compel Tancred to give back his conquests of Byzantine territory. With his hands now free, Alexius turned to diplomacy to achieve his aims. An envoy requiring Tancred to cease operations and promising him gifts was dismissed by the regent, and the emperor began to prepare for war. For this to succeed, Antioch had to be isolated as much as possible both from the other Crusader states and from Western Europe, while it was necessary either to ensure the neutrality of the Italian maritime powers or to gain them as active allies. To achieve the first aim a Byzantine envoy, previously the commander in Latakia, was sent in 1111 to Count Bertrand of Tripoli, King Baldwin I of Jerusalem and Joscelin of Courtenay, at that time the lord of the important Edessan castle of Turbessel. The mission achieved little, and ended at Easter 1112. Of greater significance were the emperor's negotiations with Pisa. Pisan ships had supported Antioch in the attempts to evict the Byzantines from Latakia in 1099 and 1108, but in 1110 Alexius's diplomacy was successful. The Pisan state swore fealty to Alexius, and in the following year received trading and other privileges from him. There was one important reservation: Pisan ships were permitted to transport pilgrims and Crusaders with their weapons provided that they swore neither to commit nor support any action in Syria against the Byzantines.

Although it seems that Alexius planned to take action against Antioch in 1113, this never happened. His plans were thrown into confusion by independent attacks from two Turcic peoples: the Seljuks of Rūm in Anatolia, and the Kipchaks of the steppes of southern Russia and the Crimea. In fact there was in 1118, the last year of Alexius's life, a reversal of Byzantine policy, when Alexius's envoy in Antioch tried to negotiate a marriage between his son and heir, John Comnenus, and a daughter of Roger of Salerno, through which Antioch would in due due course revert to the Empire. The plan collapsed with Roger's death on the Field of Blood in the following year, when the Byzantine envoy was captured. Later Alexius took up the negotiations with King Baldwin II as regent of Antioch, but the project came to nothing. John Comnenus came to the throne in 1118, but he was not able to deal with the problem of Antioch before 1135.

Jerusalem and its Muslim neighbours to 1119

The political system of Jerusalem in this early period differed greatly from that of Antioch. There was little intervention in Palestine by the

Muslim states of the north, and there was no threat from the Byzantines. Relations with Egypt were all-important since the Fatimid caliphate had an advanced base in the Palestinian littoral at Ascalon, its third *thaghr* or frontier harbour, a position shared with Rosetta and Damietta. The nascent Frankish state needed to secure its nucleus, the narrow strip of territory linking Jerusalem with Jaffa by way of al-Ramla and Lydda, and it needed also to expand to form a viable entity. The following survey of developments will therefore fall into three interconnected parts: the defence against Egypt in the south, expansion into the western coastlands, and expansion north and east into Galilee and Transjordan.

The Fatimid caliphate was at this time effectively in the hands of al-Afḍal Shāhanshāh, the son of Badr al-Jamālī, the Armenian governor of Acre who had intervened to end chaos and anarchy in Egypt and restore order in the name of the Caliph al-Mustanṣir, whose *wazīr* and commander-in-chief (*amīr al-juyūsh*) he was. Badr and al-Mustanṣir both died in 1094, and al-Afḍal installed as head of state first the late caliph's son, al-Mustaʿlī, and on his death in 1101 his infant son, al-Āmir. Al-Afḍal held virtually unchallenged sway until he was assassinated by the young caliph's order in 1121. He was therefore the primary opponent of the kingdom of Jerusalem in the opening period of its existence.

The Fatimid threat became apparent no more than three weeks after the Frankish capture of Jerusalem, when an Egyptian army, originally called in aid by the previous rulers of the city, arrived outside Ascalon. There on 12 August 1099 the Egyptians were confronted by Godfrey of Bouillon, king of Jerusalem in all but name, and routed with heavy losses. Al-Afḍal fled within the walls of Ascalon, and proceeded thence by sea to Egypt, but the city itself held out against the Franks, and was in fact to remain under Fatimid rule for another 53 years.

Al-Afḍal did not however give up his hope of driving the Franks out of Palestine. In the meantime Godfrey died, and his brother, Baldwin of Boulogne, came up from Edessa to be crowned king of Jerusalem in December 1100. On at least three occasions al-Afḍal launched attacks on the new kingdom between 1101 and 1105. The first, in September 1101, was defeated near al-Ramla. A second invasion, commanded by al-Afḍal's son, Sharaf al-Maʿālī, met with initial success. The Fatimid forces reached Lydda, burnt down the cathedral, and went on to besiege the king in al-Ramla. He escaped personally, but the town fell to the Egyptians, who next besieged Jaffa. The reappearance of the king, the arrival of relieving forces from Galilee and Jerusalem, and more significantly the arrival of a naval squadron, ended the threat. The victorious Franks went on to attempt a siege of Ascalon, which proved unsuccessful. It is reported that on this occasion al-Afḍal, the *wazīr* and protector of the Shi'i Fatimids, sought the cooperation of Dokak, the Sunni ruler of Damascus, which he failed to obtain. For his third project of invasion in 1105, al-Afḍal made a similar diplomatic overture. Dokak had died in 1104, and Tuğtigin ruled in Damascus as the *atabeg* for his infant son. The succession was however contested by Dokak's brother, who, acting in concert with the governor of Buṣrā, urged Baldwin to attack Damascus. Before settling matters with these opponents, Tuğtigin willingly cooperated with al-Afḍal, whose forces once again advanced towards al-Ramla. They were heavily defeated by Baldwin, and withdrew from the battlefield.

A period of quiet ensued on this southern front until 1118, when Baldwin planned a direct attack on Egypt. The forces he assembled were insufficient to conquer the country, still less to hold it, and it has been suggested that this was an exploratory operation or perhaps an attempt to acquire a bridgehead in Egyptian territory. Al-Faramā' was taken and sacked, and the Franks advanced towards the eastern arm of the Nile. Then Baldwin was taken ill, and he died near al-'Arīsh on the return journey. His remains were taken to Jerusalem, and buried in the Church of the Holy Sepulchre.

Expansion into the coastlands of Palestine was essential to the new kingdom of Jerusalem for two reasons. In the first place, the Crusaders were a land-based force, and had no fleet of their own. They were thus dependent on the ships of others, in effect almost exclusively on the Italian maritime republics, and it was they who conveyed pilgrims and provisions to the Holy Land. Hence it was absolutely essential for the Franks to capture and hold the coastal towns and harbours of Palestine. As it was, these towns either were or had been Fatimid possessions, and their Muslim inhabitants were potential collaborators with Egyptian land forces in attacks on the Franks. On the other hand, since these ports were the natural and traditional outlets for the commerce of the hinterland, their seizure by the Franks was a factor in promoting cooperation between the Sunni and Turkish-ruled states of Syria and the Shi'i Fatimid caliphate of Egypt.

Expansion into the coastlands followed quickly on the establishment of the Frankish state. Haifa, at the time a small town of minor importance, was taken in August 1100 with the help of Venetian ships. Caesarea was captured in the following month with Genoese aid, and a massacre took place. Arsūf, which had paid tribute to the Franks since 1099, revolted, and was finally subdued in April 1101 by Baldwin I in cooperation with a Genoese fleet. Here also a massacre occurred. In 1103 Baldwin attempted to take the dominant harbour-city of Acre. His first attempt failed, but then he secured Genoese help. The Fatimid governor fled to Damascus, and the city capitulated in May 1104. The terms of the capitulation were dishonoured, and once again a massacre was perpetrated. It is significant that the fall of Acre was followed by cooperation between al-Afḍal (who had been born in the city) and Tuğtigin in the campaign of 1105, as mentioned earlier. The northward expansion up the coast was resumed in 1108, when Baldwin unsuccessfully besieged Sidon, which already paid him tribute. Operations against Beirut were more fortunate. The Fatimid governor fled, the city fell in May 1110, and the people were massacred (against the king's orders) by men from the Pisan and Genoese ships that had assisted him. A second siege of Sidon, later in the same year, succeeded as Baldwin had the support of Norwegian ships under King Sigurd, a Venetian fleet, and the newly established Count Bertrand of Tripoli. The judge of Sidon negotiated a safe conduct to Damascus in December 1110, and some 5,000 people evacuated the city. The agreement was respected by the Franks, but Baldwin laid a crippling indemnity on those who remained in Sidon and its neighbourhood. Tyre remained untaken until 1124, although it was menaced from about 1105 by the building of the castle of Toron (Arabic, Tibnīn) in the Galilean hills above the coastland.

To the north of these ports lay the important city of Tripoli, which had a history of its own. After the death of its last Fatimid governor, the Shiʿi judge, Amīn al-Dawla Ibn ʿAmmār, proclaimed the city's independence, and became its ruler. He sought the support of the Fatimids' chief rival, Tuğtigin, but had to act cautiously in order to preserve his independence of both powers and to conciliate the people of Tripoli, who were largely Fatimid sympathisers. This policy was followed by his two successors, Jalāl al-Mulk Ibn ʿAmmār (1072–99) and Fakhr al-Mulk Ibn ʿAmmār (1099–1109). Raymond of Saint-Gilles, who had at one time been seen as the leader of the Crusade and potential ruler of Jerusalem, was forced to satisfy himself with the taking in 1102 of Tortosa (Anṭarṭūs), about 45 km up the coast from Tripoli, and the anticipated capture of Tripoli itself, of which he began to style himself the count in 1103. His castle, built on Mount Pilgrim, blocked the landward approaches, but he died in 1105 with the city itself still under siege. When it fell to his former troops in 1109, Fakhr al-Mulk Ibn ʿAmmār negotiated a safe conduct to Damascus for himself and his people. The succession to Raymond was disputed between the supporters of his cousin, William Jordan, and his eldest son, Bertrand of Toulouse, who arrived in Syria. A council of the Crusader princes under Baldwin imposed a partition of the territory, which soon ended when William Jordan died from an arrow-wound. The new county was constituted a fief of Jerusalem.

The northern and eastern extension of the kingdom of Jerusalem itself was initially the work of Tancred of Hauteville, who assumed the title of 'prince of Galilee' and established himself at Tiberias and Baysān, where the long valley below the Carmel ridge runs down to the Jordan. The inhabitants of Galilee – Muslims, Oriental Christians and Jews – quietly accepted their Norman overlord, who continued the expansion of his lands to the eastern side of the Sea of Galilee. Here lay the territory known as al-Sawād, Terre de Saete to the Franks, good grazing country, where Tancred established his supremacy against an opponent known only by his Frankish appellation of *Grossus Rusticus*, 'the Big Peasant'. A direct clash with Damascus, still ruled by Dokak, ensued, but was a failure. Tancred's intention to dominate Transjordan south of the Yarmūk, the Biblical Gilead, designated Jabal 'Awf, was cut short when he was summoned to rule Antioch as Bohemond's regent. Tancred transferred his possessions in Galilee to Baldwin in 1101, at first conditionally on his return, and it was Baldwin who consolidated the control of the territories lying east of the Jordan and the Dead Sea. His advance in this region was secured in 1115 by the building of a castle known as Montréal at al-Shawbak in the hills south-east of the Dead Sea, and he penetrated further south to the head of the gulf of 'Aqaba and the island of al-Quraya, known to the Franks as Ile de Graye. The domination of Transjordan was particularly important to Baldwin and his successors as it enabled them to intercept the great trade route from Damascus to Egypt, which with its branch to the Hijaz was also the pilgrimage route to Mecca. To complete the story, it should be added that in 1142 Pagan the Butler, the lord of Transjordan, built the castle of Krak des Moabites at al-Karak, east of the Dead Sea and three days' march from Montréal. A town grew up around the castle, and the site had a long history.

An interesting feature of these years was the formal recognition of a balance of power between Baldwin I and Tuğtigin in two frontier areas, which was signalled by the conclusion of an armistice and an agreement for the sharing of revenues. The first of these is noted in the *Damascus Chronicle* for AH 502 (11 August 1108 to 30 July 1109)[1] in the following words:

> In this year a number of envoys from King Baldwin came to Ẓahīr al-Dīn [Tuğtigin] with proposals for an armistice and the establishment of amicable relations. An arrangement was reached between them that the Sawād and Jabal 'Awf should be divided into thirds, the Turks [i.e. Tuğtigin] to have one-third, and the Franks [i.e. Baldwin] and the peasantry two-thirds. The compact was concluded on this proposition, and the terms written down on this basis.[2]

The situation was more complex in another region, the Biqāʿ, la Boquée to the Franks, the fertile vale lying between the ranges of Lebanon and Anti-Lebanon with Baʿlabakk as its chief town. This area was frequently raided by the Franks, and Tuğtigin sought a settlement with Baldwin I in AH 503 (31 July 1109 to 19 July 1310), as is mentioned in the *Damascus Chronicle*:

> There passed between them [i.e. the Franks] and Ẓahīr al-Dīn some correspondence and negotiations, which led to both parties agreeing to make an amicable settlement regarding their territories and to establish peaceful relations. A treaty was concluded on the terms that the Franks should receive one-third of the produce of the Biqāʿ and that the centres of al-Munaitira and Ibn ʿAkkār should be delivered up to them, that they should abstain from their plundering and ravaging in the provinces and outlying districts, that the castles of Masyāf Hisn al-Tufan and Hisn al-Akrād should be included in the terms of the treaty, and that their inhabitants should pay a stipulated sum annually to the Franks as protection-money. The Franks observed these conditions for a short time, but they did not long continue within the terms of the agreement and returned to their customary ravaging and destroying.[3]

There was in fact more at issue than border raiding. Some time later, probably towards the end of 1109, Tuğtigin heard that the governor of Baʿlabakk, the eunuch Gümüştigin al-Tājī, had sent envoys to urge the Franks to raid the border districts, and had also sent his brother to stir up trouble for Tuğtigin at the sultan's court. This led Tuğtigin to mount a punitive expedition against Gümüştigin, and Baʿlabakk surrendered on 14 April 1110. Although the chronicler does not make the connection, this treachery may have occasioned an undated raid by Baldwin in the same year and the resultant settlement as recorded in the *Damascus Chronicle*:

> In this year also King Baldwin, lord of Jerusalem, arrived in the district of Baʿlabakk with the object of plundering and creating devastation in the district of the Biqāʿ. A correspondence ensued between them and Ẓahīr al-Dīn Atābak in regard to this, until it was agreed to establish amicable relations between them on the condition that one-third of the produce of the Biqāʿ should belong to the Franks, and two-thirds to the Muslims and the peasantry. A protocol was drawn up between them on these terms in Ṣafar of this year, and he set off to return to his own province, retaining possession of the plunder from Baʿlabakk and the Biqāʿ which was in his hands and the hands of his troops.[4]

These instruments in fact created a condominium over the regions concerned, although the Arabic term for condominium (*munāṣafa*) is not used here. There is an ambiguity about the date of the protocol.

Ibn al-Qalānisī dates it 'in Ṣafar of the year', which Gibb renders more precisely as 'of this year'. Gibb notes however that it should probably be dated in Ṣafar 504, beginning 19 August 1110.

Frankish and Muslim military and naval forces

It is time now to consider more closely the military relations between the alien Frankish implant in the Near East and its Muslim neighbours. There were at times pitched battles, and it is possible to pick out a series of these high points of hostility: the Field of Blood (1119), Inab (1149) and Ḥaṭṭīn (1187). These were not however usually characteristic of Frankish–Muslim hostilities, in which raiding on a larger or smaller scale was more common, resulting in the taking of cattle or hostages. Where there was no clear borderline between a Frankish and a Muslim ruler because of their balance of power, the result, as has just been seen, was a condominium with the rivals sharing the revenues of the disputed territories. These condominia were transitory arrangements, the symptoms of a nascent shift of power. They appear in the twelfth century when the Franks were establishing their borders, and again in the Mamluk–Frankish treaties of the late thirteenth century as a stage in the Muslim reconquest.

What was at stake in hostilities was security of territory – the control of the strategic points that gave safety and viability to tracts of land. The strategic points were of two kinds, the cities and the castles. Many of the cities were very ancient, such as Damascus, Tyre and Sidon. These were places in which a full urban life was possible, sustained by the activities of ports and markets. A contrasting example is offered by al-Manṣūra, about 61 km south of Damietta on the river, which originated in an encampment of Egyptian forces in the resistance to the Fifth Crusade and the Crusade of St Louis, and developed into a full town.

Castles became numerous during the Crusading period through the activities of the Frankish military orders. The first order to appear was that of the Templars, an organisation of knights formed to defend the Holy Land against the Muslims. They took their name from 'Solomon's Temple', as the Franks called the mosque of al-Aqṣā in Jerusalem, which King Baldwin II gave to these knights as their residence and headquarters. They could contribute perhaps 300 men to the fighting forces of the kingdom, but their chief duty was to garrison their castles. The second of the great military orders was that of the Hospital. This developed from a religious complex founded in Jerusalem before the First Crusade by merchants from Amalfi, which included a hospital for pilgrims dedicated to St John the Baptist. By 1143 at the latest, staff of the Hospital were patrolling the routes to Jerusalem to ensure the safety of pilgrims. As its military functions increased, the Hospital established and garrisoned castles throughout the Holy Land. When the Templars were suppressed by Pope Clement V in 1312, their castles passed to the Hospitallers. The third great military order was that of the Teutonic Knights, which developed in 1098 from a field hospital for German pilgrims. Its principal castle was Starkenburg (Arabic, al-Qurayn) in the hills between Acre and Tyre.

For raiding or for fighting pitched battles, both the Frankish and the Muslim states had their armed forces, in which the mounted warrior was of chief importance. The Frankish rulers depended in the first place on their feudal vassals, the knights, whose ancestors had come out as Crusaders and settled in the Holy Land. Like the knights in Western Europe, they subsisted on the fiefs granted them by the rulers. Unlike knights in Europe however, they did not usually dwell on their fiefs, forming a local aristocracy or gentry, since the land was still worked by the indigenous peasantry and its Frankish lords lived by preference in the safer and more congenial cities. Their adoption of local styles of clothing and other native usages provoked the scornful disapproval of pilgrims and other newly arrived Westerners. Moreover since the land available for distribution in fiefs was limited, and since the Near East was accustomed to a money economy far in advance of Western Europe, many vassals were provided with money fiefs – grants levied on urban rents and properties.

The forces of a Frankish ruler needed to be increased from other sources, and so there was a continuous recruitment of mercenaries. These might be Christians, frequently Armenians, while the Maronites of Lebanon gave considerable assistance to their neighbours in the county of Tripoli. Particularly important among the mercenaries were the *turcoples*, natives of the Holy Land who served as light cavalry or mounted archers. The military orders acted independently of the Frankish rulers, but were usually prepared to cooperate with them in joint enterprises. Finally, there were visiting Crusaders, who came out from Europe during the fighting season from spring to autumn. Some of them stayed and settled in the Holy Land, and might be regarded as unwelcome interlopers. Perhaps the most famous of these is Reynald of Châtillon.

As the Frankish ruler depended primarily on his feudal host, so did his Muslim counterpart on his corps of mounted guards, his *ʿaskar*. These were usually Turkish military slaves, i.e. *mamlūk*s, who had been brought as boys from their homelands beyond the eastern frontiers of Islam or from the Kipchak steppe north of the Black Sea. The commander of the whole corps usually bore the title of *ḥājib* (chamberlain), and each component regiment was headed by an amir. An amir had also usually his personal body of guardsmen, who derived their name from his cognomen, for example the Asadiyya of Asad al-Dīn Shīrkūh and the Ṣalāḥiyya of Saladin (Ṣalāḥ al-Dīn). The maintenance of amirs and their troops was provided by the grant of *iqṭā*ʿs, a term often mistranslated as 'fiefs'. The two institutions were similar in function but their origins were very different. The *iqṭā*ʿ, a product of the Near Eastern money economy, was the assignment of the revenue of a district to an amir, who safeguarded his income by having also the powers of a governor over the district. Beside the *ʿaskar*, a second line of cavalry was provided by the *jund* (plural, *ajnād*), a local territorial mounted militia, and as such a force of freemen, not *mamlūk*s. There were also locally levied foot soldiers, who played a minor part in campaigns.

There was no counterpart to the military orders on the Muslim side, but the ruler could count on the aid of mercenary troops. These were both Muslims and Christians, and included Turcomans (always a restless and troublesome element in the Fertile Crescent), Daylamīs, an Iranian people from the highlands south of the Caspian Sea, and the ubiquitous Armenians. Even before the emergence of Saladin and his Ayyubid kin, the Kurds were recruited both to the *ʿaskar*s and as auxiliary cavalry.

In conflict the cavalry charge was the decisive manoeuvre for both sides, but tactics varied. The Frankish charger was a large and heavy horse, and was used after a preliminary shower of arrows to bear down upon and break through the ranks of the enemy, the knights using their lances and then their swords. The Muslims used their lighter steeds to perform a different manoeuvre known as *al-karr wa'l-farr*, i.e. attacking and retreating. The Muslim cavalry would make or feign an attack and then retreat, hoping to tempt the enemy out of his fixed position and then to fall upon him. It was a tactic that gave the advantage to the lightly armed Muslim horsemen and was puzzling to the Franks, whose experience in Europe was an enemy armed and mounted like themselves.

The intrusion of the Franks into the Near East during the First Crusade took the Muslims by surprise, and this assisted the intruders. In the long run however the situation of the Franks was precarious. Their numbers were never large and in their states they were alien rulers and settlers, dominating a sullen and irreconcilable population.

The Crusaders were land-based warriors who never possessed sea power. For the capture and exploitation of the ports and harbours of Syria-Palestine they depended upon cooperation with the fleets of the Italian merchant republics. From the first establishment of the Frankish states, the Italians played a prominent part in their affairs. When Godfrey of Bouillon ruled Jerusalem in 1100, he endeavoured to weaken his opponent Daimbert, archbishop of Pisa and patriarch of Jerusalem, by granting Venice, Pisa's rival, freedom to trade throughout the kingdom and a third of every town the Venetians helped the Crusaders to capture. The Genoese aided Godfrey's successor, King Baldwin I, to capture Arsūf and Caesarea in 1101 and the important port of Acre in 1104. Baldwin's taking of Sidon and Beirut was assisted not by the Italians but by a strange fleet in Mediterranean waters, that of King Sigurd of Norway, whose expedition is commemorated by the Icelandic historian, Snorri Sturluson, who wrote in his *Heimskringla* in the first half of the thirteenth century:

> In summer King Sigurd sailed across the Greek sea to Palestine, and came to Acre, where he landed, and went by land to Jerusalem. King Baldwin received him particularly well, and rode with him all the way to the river Jordan, and then back to the city of Jerusalem . . . King Sigurd stayed a long time in the land of Jerusalem in autumn, and in the beginning of winter.
>
> King Baldwin made a magnificent feast for King Sigurd and many of his people, and gave him many holy relics. [The relics included a splinter from the wood of the Cross.] After this King Sigurd returned to his ships at Acre; and then King Baldwin prepared to go to Syria, to a town called Saet, which some think had been Sidon. This castle, which belonged to the heathens, he wished to conquer, and lay under the Christians. On this expedition King Sigurd accompanied him with all his men, and sixty ships; and after the kings had besieged the town some time it surrendered, and they took possession of it. The kings took the city itself and the troops all the other booty. King Sigurd made a present of his share to King Baldwin.
>
> . . . Thereafter King Sigurd went to his ships, and made ready to leave Palestine.[5]

Sigurd's crusading expedition was in 1110. In the previous year the Genoese and Provençal fleets had enabled the Crusaders to capture the city of Tripoli, long blockaded on the landward side by Raymond of Saint-Gilles, who died in 1105.

Among the Muslim powers in the Near East, the Fatimids alone had paid attention to sea power. They developed an effective navy, which contributed to the Fatimid conquest of Egypt in 969. By the time of the Crusades the Fatimid navy was in decline and was unable to offer much opposition to the Italian fleets. After Saladin's acquisition of Egypt a revival took place. A naval department (*dīwān al-usṭūl*) was set up, and the financial support for its activities increased. When Reynald of Châtillon tried in 1183 to build a fleet in the Red Sea and threaten the coast of Arabia (see Chapter 4), Saladin's naval forces delivered a crushing response. On the other hand, they were unable to intercept European access by sea to the Frankish states, and in the end this Muslim navy was virtually destroyed during the siege of Acre in the Third Crusade. Its passing marks the end of Near Eastern Muslim attempts to acquire sea power before the rise of the Ottoman Empire.

Notes

1. AH signifies *Anno Hegirae*, 'in the year of Hijra', i.e. the emigration of the Prophet Muḥammed from Mecca to Medina (AD 622), the starting point of the Muslim calendar.
2. Gibb, *Damascus Chronicle*, p. 92. In this and the two following excerpts some diacritics have been added.
3. Gibb, *Damascus Chronicle*, p. 93.
4. Gibb, *Damascus Chronicle*, p. 106.
5. Snorri Sturluson, *Heimskringla*, tr. Samuel Laing, London: Everyman's Library, 1961, pp. 282–4.

chapter three

FROM THE FIELD OF BLOOD TO THE SECOND CRUSADE: 1119–49

At the age of nearly 70, Fulcher of Chartres, who had been present at the Council of Clermont and had accompanied the Crusaders, completed in 1127 or 1128 his chronicle of events, and depicted the Holy Land as a place of settlement, its people quiet and self-confident after victory:

> Consider, I pray, and reflect how in our time God has transferred the West into the East. For we who were Occidentals now have been made Orientals. He who was a Roman or a Frank is now a Galilean or an inhabitant of Palestine. One who was a citizen of Rheims or of Chartres now has been made a citizen of Tyre or of Antioch. We have already forgotten the places of our birth; already they have become unbeknown to many of us, or, at least, are unmentioned. Some already possess here homes and servants which they have received through inheritance. Some have taken wives not merely of their own people, but Syrians, or Armenians, or even Saracens who have received the grace of baptism. Some have with them father-in-law, or daughter-in-law, or son-in-law, or step-son, or step-father. There are here, too, grandchildren and great-grandchildren. One cultivates vines, another the fields. The one and the other use mutually the speech and the idioms of the different languages. Different languages, now made common, become known to both races, and faith unites those whose forefathers were strangers. As it is written, 'The lion and the ox shall eat straw together'. Those who were strangers are now natives; and he who was a sojourner now has become a resident. Our parents and relatives from day to day come to join us, abandoning, even though reluctantly, all that they possess. For those who were poor there, here God makes rich.[1]

This may seem an over-optimistic and exaggerated picture of the fusion of peoples and cultures some 30 years after the Crusaders took Antioch. Its unconscious irony will indeed become apparent in this chapter as it moves between the two greatest calamities suffered by the Franks in their first half-century: the Field of Blood in 1119, when the forces of Antioch and their ruler succumbed to İlgazi the Artukid, and the more comprehensive failure of the Second Crusade outside Damascus in 1149. These years saw a reassertion of Muslim power in the Syrian-Palestinian borderlands, and with it a change in the relationship of the Muslims with the Frankish states. They had however one neighbour that was not Muslim, the Byzantine Empire, which throughout this period was ruled by three powerful and active members of the Comneni family: Alexius I (1081–1118), his son John II (1118–43) and his grandson Manuel I (1143–80). It is to the Byzantine factor in the affairs of the Frankish states that we must first turn.

The Byzantine factor

Two matters affected the relations between the Byzantines and the Franks. One was the standing problem of the Byzantine claim to Antioch, never withdrawn although set aside by Bohemond's creation of 'facts on the ground'. Behind it lay a wider but more shadowy assertion of rights to Edessa and even to all the long-lost provinces of the Eastern Roman Empire in Syria and Palestine. Second, the Frankish states were continually dependent on the Byzantine navy, as on other Christian fleets in eastern waters, to keep open their communications with the West so that pilgrims and other potential settlers could augment the sparse Frankish population and contribute to its military strength. But neither party was acting freely in these matters. Both were involved in relationships with various European powers – the Italian maritime states such as Pisa, Venice and Genoa, the Normans of southern Italy and Sicily, the papacy, and the Germans with their imperial ambitions also in Italy. It is against a tangled web of diplomacy, armed peace and open warfare that the workings of the Byzantine factor in Crusader history must be viewed.

The Comneni pursued their claim to Antioch and other Crusader territories by various means – diplomacy, projects of dynastic marriages, and force or the threat of force. In 1108 Alexius had defeated Bohemond in Europe and compelled him to accept the Treaty of Devol. Although their agreements of 1097 were declared invalid, Bohemond had to profess himself the liege vassal of Alexius and John Comnenus. It was laid down that after his death his principality was to revert to the Byzantine Empire, while he was not to occupy without the emperor's agreement any former Byzantine territories he might conquer. Should he rebel against the emperor, his vassals were freed from their obligations towards him. He undertook to compel Tancred, his regent in Antioch, to end his hostility to the emperor, and he promised to restore to the Empire his conquests in Cilicia as well as the coastal cities such as Latakia, Jabala and Anṭarṭūs. Although Bohemond claimed that Edessa was under the suzerainty of Antioch, he was not conceded any right to dispose of it. While this settlement was concluded between Alexius and Bohemond, Tancred remained as the actual ruler of Antioch, and he was the Emperor's irreconcilable opponent.

When in 1108 and 1109 successful campaigns by Tancred brought Latakia and western Syria under his control, Alexius called on him to respect the Devol settlement. Tancred rejected the demand, and the two powers were brought to the edge of hostilities. Alexius however dared not go to war without first isolating Antioch from the other Frankish states and securing the neutrality, if not the support, of the Italian maritime cities and the other Western powers. This he partially accomplished in the following years by diplomatic means, and it seems that operations against Antioch were planned to take place in 1113. The blow never fell, as Alexius was then distracted by more immediate threats: the incursions of the Rūm Seljuks into Anatolia, followed by an invasion of the Cumans across the northern frontier of the Empire in Europe. At the end of Alexius's life, he made an attempt to secure Antioch by other means. Tancred died in 1112, and was succeeded by his nephew, Roger of the Principate. The new ruler received an envoy from Alexius in 1118 with a proposal for the marriage of Roger's daughter to a Byzantine prince, namely John Comnenus or (more probably) his son. The matter was still in suspense when Roger was amongst those killed on the Field of Blood in 1119, by which time John had succeeded to the Empire. The regent of Antioch after Roger's death, King Baldwin II, was uninterested in the marriage project.

Under John II Comnenus the confrontation that had developed between Alexius and the rulers of Antioch reached a climax. King Baldwin's regency ended in 1126 when Bohemond II, the son of the founder of the principality, came to Antioch as its ruler. He married Baldwin's daughter, Alice, on his arrival. Bohemond II showed himself to be a warrior prince like his father, and endeavoured to re-establish the eastern frontier against Aleppo, where there had been losses after the Field of Blood. His reign and his life were cut short in 1130, when he was perhaps 21 years old. He was killed in battle near Mopsuestia in Cilicia, the modern Turkish Misis. His heir was his two-year-old daughter, Constance.

Who was now to rule the principality? It was claimed for a time by the king of Sicily, Roger II, as head of the house of Hauteville, but difficulties in Europe prevented him from pressing his claim. The Princess Alice, Constance's mother, endeavoured unsuccessfully to rule. The regency ultimately fell in 1131 to Baldwin's successor, his son-in-law Fulk of

Anjou, who became king of Jerusalem in 1131 in right of his wife, Melisende. In 1136 Fulk sent to Antioch as his deputy Raymond of Poitou, a son of the duke of Aquitaine. In the previous year Alice had proposed the betrothal of Constance to Manuel, the youngest son of John Comnenus. As in 1118, this proposal raised the prospect of the peaceful reabsorption of Antioch into the Byzantine Empire. It was to prove equally illusory. On his arrival, Raymond was betrothed to Constance without Alice's knowledge, thus checkmating both the Byzantine marriage alliance and Alice's hope of maintaining control over the principality.

John Comnenus thereupon turned to the option of using armed force against Antioch and its new ruler. His operations began in 1137 with a campaign in Cilicia, a region where Frankish power was predominant in the west, while the Armenians controlled the east. The Byzantine forces assembled at Attalia (now Antalya) in the south of Asia Minor, and then advanced along the coastal road to Seleucia (now Silifke). Corycus was the first Frankish possession to fall to the Byzantines, who pressed on to take the important cities of Tarsus, Adana and Mopsuestia lying in the Cilician plain. Further conquests followed in Armenian Cilicia, where the fortress city of Anazarbus (now Anavarza, north-east of Tarsus) was taken after months of fighting, followed by the fall of Tall Ḥamdūn (now Toprakkale), about 29 km east of Adana. John made a thrust to the north of Armenian Cilicia, which however resulted in no further conquest. Having thus secured their communications, the Byzantines turned southwards to Antioch, where they arrived in August 1137, and placed the city under siege. The other Frankish states could give no effective help, and negotiations ended in a compromise. Raymond declared himself the emperor's liegeman and promised to restore Antioch to the emperor, if John for his part would grant him the lordship of Aleppo, Shayzar, Ḥamāh and Ḥimṣ. To this exchange the emperor agreed. There were however two difficulties. The promised territories were all under Muslim rule, Zangī notably being the lord of Aleppo, and the year was too advanced to allow John and Raymond to set out against them. The campaign was therefore postponed until the spring of 1138.

At the end of the campaigning season of 1137 the Byzantine forces withdrew to winter quarters in Cilicia, and here John took the opportunity to complete the operations anticipated by his northward thrust before his descent on Antioch. He besieged and took the stronghold of Vahka (now Feke), and made captive its Armenian lord, Leon, who was the head of the Roupenids, one of the two chief Armenian clans. Leon died in Constantinople, but his son, Toros, returned after John's death in 1145 and resumed Armenian resistance to the Byzantines.

When 1138 came, a combined force of Byzantines and troops from Antioch and Edessa set out to combat the Muslims in the lands promised to Raymond. The Byzantines attacked Aleppo, but their water supplies were insufficient and they were forced to break off the siege after three days. Shayzar, a fortress city under the hereditary lordship of the Arab Banū Munqidh, was next attacked by the allies. In fact the emperor alone was active in the operations, while Raymond of Antioch and Joscelin II of Edessa spent their time dicing in their tents. The lower city of Shayzar was taken without difficulty, but the citadel was a different proposition. After a siege that lasted from 20 April to 21 May 1138, John was offered an indemnity by the ruling amir to obtain his withdrawal. He accepted without consulting his allies, and returned to Antioch. He made a triumphal entry into the city and there were protracted and unsuccessful negotiations about the future of his agreement with Raymond. Finally John, who was anxious about safety in Antioch, returned to his army encamped outside. After a meaningless reconciliation with the rulers of Antioch and Edessa, the emperor made his way back to Constantinople.

Although to John's mind there was still unfinished business in Antioch, more urgent matters of diplomacy and military affairs prevented him from resuming the offensive until 1142. Then once again he advanced from Attalia into Cilicia. Thence he marched on Turbessel (Tall Bāshir in Arabic, Tellbasar in modern Turkey), a castle west of the Euphrates where Joscelin was in residence. John demanded hostages to secure Joscelin's good behaviour during the forthcoming clash with Antioch. On the way to Antioch the emperor sent an envoy to demand the surrender of the city so that he might fight the Muslims of the interior. Once again there were protracted negotiations, while John's troops plundered the suburbs. But it was now autumn, and John withdrew to winter quarters in Cilicia. Before he could resume the campaign he died in a hunting accident. His son and successor, Manuel Comnenus, returned to Constantinople, and Antioch was saved. A period of détente began under the new emperor in 1145, when Raymond went to the Byzantine capital to renew his oath of fealty.

The career of Zangī and the fall of Edessa: 1119–44

Baldwin II, count of Edessa, who became King Baldwin II of Jerusalem in 1118, appointed his supporter, Joscelin of Courtenay, as count of Edessa. As Tripoli was already a fief of Jerusalem, Baldwin as temporary regent of Antioch after the Field of Blood had the oversight for the time being of all the Frankish states. Nevertheless his control was limited, even over the royal vassals, and the problem of relations with the neighbouring Muslim states remained. In Egypt, the *wazīr* al-Afḍal was assassinated in 1121 on the orders of his ambitious young master, the Caliph al-Āmir. Tyre, the most northerly Fatimid coastal stronghold in Syria, was besieged, and it finally fell to the Franks in 1124. The capitulation included a safe conduct for those inhabitants who wished to leave, but a majority of the local population chose to stay.

The defeat of Antioch on the Field of Blood had been inflicted, as has been seen, by the Artukid İlgazi, lord of Mardin. He had been called in by Aleppo, which he continued to hold until his death in 1122, and he was succeeded there by his nephew Balak. As hostilities continued between Balak and the Franks, he captured both Joscelin of Edessa and Baldwin II in 1123. While Joscelin succeeded in escaping, Baldwin was held captive until Balak's death in 1124. At this moment of weakness, Baldwin besieged Aleppo with the support of the forces of Antioch and Edessa. In desperation, the authorities of Aleppo called in as their protector the *atabeg* of Mosul, Aksungur al-Bursuqī. The northern union that had existed under Mawdūd from 1108 to 1113 was thus recreated. The Frankish attempt to take Aleppo failed, as also did an attack on Damascus in January 1126. In November of that year Aksungur al-Bursuqī was assassinated like Mawdūd before him, and the link between Mosul and Aleppo was severed.

Its restoration was to be accomplished under a man of Turkish origin who had for some time been rising into prominence. This was Zangī, whose father, Qāsim al-Dawla Aksungur al-Ḥājib, was a *mamlūk* and friend of the Seljuk sultan, Malik-Shāh. Aksungur al-Ḥājib played an important part during Malik-Shāh's reign (1072–92), ruling in his name over northern Syria from Aleppo. During the succession troubles after Malik-Shāh's death, Aksungur at first supported his immediate Seljuk overlord, Malik-Shāh's brother Tutuş, but when it came to a battle in 1093 between Tutuş and Berkyaruk, the late sultan's eldest son, Aksungur, changed sides. Tutuş escaped defeat by flight, and in due course avenged himself on Aksungur, who was captured and put to death in 1094. His son Zangī was then perhaps seven years old.

The governor of Mosul, who had been an ally of Aksungur, regained his capital in 1096 after various vicissitudes during the reign of Tutuş. This was Kırboğa, who, two years later, led an army in an unsuccessful attempt to relieve Antioch. He now won the support of many of Aksungur's former *mamlūk*s, and adopted Zangī to strengthen his own position. Kırboğa's death in 1101 brought political changes to Mosul. Among other competitors for the possession of this key city was Tutuş's son Dokak, the lord of Damascus. Then in 1108 Sultan Tapar, the Seljuk suzerain, appointed Mawdūd as *atabeg* of Mosul. Zangī, who had been acquiring military training and experience from Kırboğa's time onwards, gave Mawdūd active support, and thereby signalled his loyalty to the Seljuks. He particularly distinguished himself during operations against King Baldwin I in 1112–13. Threatened by the Franks, Tuğtigin of Damascus sought help from Mawdūd. Their two forces combined in the Biqāʿ and moved into Galilee, driving the Franks towards Tiberias. Although the Franks were defeated, a body of survivors held out in the hills above Tiberias until the heat forced the Muslims to withdraw in August 1113.

The next phase of Zangī's career was spent in Iraq. In 1123 he was appointed to govern Wāsiṭ, south of Baghdad, and the great southern port of al-Baṣra. The Seljuk Sultan, Tapar's son Maḥmūd, who had come to the throne in 1118, also appointed him as *shiḥna* (in effect, military governor) of Baghdad. It looked as if this region was to be the setting for Zangī's later career, but this was not to be.

Aksungur al-Bursuqī, the *atabeg*, was assassinated in November 1126. His son, ʿIzz al-Dīn Masʿūd, whom he had appointed to govern Aleppo, returned to Mosul as his successor. In 1127 he died in a campaign against Tuğtigin of Damascus, and his son was proclaimed to succeed him. Two of the envoys sent to the sultan to obtain his official appointment thought otherwise however, and put forward the name of Zangī as a strong man with the ability to defend Islam. Their suggestion could not have been unacceptable to Sultan Maḥmūd, who thereupon appointed Zangī as *atabeg* of Mosul. He entered his new capital in September or October 1127, and Aleppo in June 1128. With these two cities as his base he was to go on to further successes.

During the following years Zangī's activities were to be divided among matters arising from his tenure of Mosul, the most important city in northern Mesopotamia, and Aleppo, the chief city in northern Syria, and he was also involved in the politics of his overlord, the Seljuk sultan, and the head of Sunni Islam, the ʿAbbasid caliph of Baghdad. It is however his concern with the warfare and politics of his Muslim and Frankish neighbours in Syria-Palestine that are particularly important here.

In the dozen years that followed Zangī's appointment to Aleppo he was chiefly occupied in Syria with extending his possessions and power to the south. Above all he wished to gain Damascus, which would make him paramount in Muslim Syria and the immediate neighbour of the kingdom of Jerusalem. At the outset the odds seemed in his favour. The *Atabeg* Tuğtigin, the vigorous opponent of the Franks, died on 11 February 1128, and was succeeded by his son Tāj al-Mulūk Böri, in Arabic script Būrī, whence the dynasty is styled the Burids.

At this point a new group in Syria came to dominate the affairs of Damascus. The Isma'ilis, originally an offshoot of the Fatimid Shi'is, had developed as an extremist sect in Iran. Their headquarters was the stronghold of Alamūt, which they occupied in 1090, and they were led by a succession of teachers of their faith, which they called the New Summons (*al-Daʿwa al-Jadīda*). A terrorist organisation, which was under their control and came to be known as the Assassins, was used against their opponents. In the wake of the fragmentation of Seljuk power and the impact of the Crusaders, Syria formed a favourable region for the establishment of this movement. At first it was known to ordinary Muslims and Franks chiefly through a number of terrorist killings (literally assassinations), of which the victims were prominent Muslims such as Mawdūd in 1113 and Aksungur al-Bursuqī in 1126.

For a time the Isma'ilis were dominant in Damascus, and towards the end of Tuğtigin's life they established a headquarters there. After his death they secretly conspired with the Franks to surrender Damascus in exchange for Tyre at an agreed date in September 1129. Word of this came to Böri, who struck first. The *wazīr* of Damascus, who sponsored the Isma'ilis, was killed, and they themselves were slaughtered in a popular rising. Frankish forces, which had mustered in the kingdom of Jerusalem, advanced to Bāniyās, a town that Tuğtigin had given to the Isma'ilis. Then they marched on Damascus but withdrew after a few days, fearing that their line of communications would be cut. In the following years the Isma'ilis found a new base in the hill country of Jabal Bahrā' (now Jabal Anṣāriyya), where they acquired a number of strongholds.

At the beginning of 1130 Zangī went to Aleppo and called on Böri for help in the *jihād*. Böri responded by sending one of his sons, the governor of Ḥamāh, with a contingent of 500 horsemen. They were seized on their arrival and sent to Mosul, while Zangī demanded a large sum for their release. In the meantime he took Ḥamāh, besieged Ḥimṣ without success, and finally returned to Mosul.

For the next four years from 1130 to 1133 Zangī was occupied elsewhere, but an event occurred that was to be of significance for the future. Sultan Maḥmūd died in September 1131 and in the ensuing competition among his brothers over the succession Zangī supported Mas'ūd. Intercepted and suffering a military rebuff, Zangī was enabled to cross the Tigris to safety by the Kurdish governor of Takrīt, Najm al-Dīn Ayyūb. Such was the first meeting of the founders of the Zangid and Ayyubid dynasties.

In May 1131 Böri fell victim to an attack by two Iranian assassins. His wounds were not immediately fatal but he died in June 1132. His successor was his son, the *Atabeg* Shams al-Mulūk Ismā'īl, who regained

Ḥamāh in 1133. Thereafter his rule proved disastrous. He was unpopular and in 1134 called on Zangī for help, promising to surrender Damascus to him. He disregarded the remonstrances of his mother, Ṣafwat al-Mulk Zumurrud Hatun, who procured his murder and the appointment of another of her sons, Shihāb al-Dīn Maḥmūd, as *atabeg*. In mid-February 1135 Zangī brought his army up to Damascus, encountered unexpected resistance, and settled down to besiege the city. Some weeks later an envoy arrived from the 'Abbasid Caliph al-Mustarshid recalling Zangī to Mosul. Zangī broke off the siege, and withdrew on 17 March 1135.

Zangī's next Syrian campaign was in 1137, and his immediate objective was to besiege Ḥimṣ. But while engaged on the siege he heard that a Frankish force led by the king of Jerusalem, Fulk of Anjou, was advancing on Ḥamāh. A victory here would cut Zangī's communications with Aleppo, but the Franks were forced to secure themselves in the stronghold of Montferrand, where they were besieged by Zangī. Meanwhile in August 1137 relieving forces advanced from Jerusalem and Tripoli, and the besiegers learned that John Comnenus was at Antioch. Faced by the prospect of Byzantine assistance to the Franks, Zangī decided to negotiate with King Fulk, and the troops were allowed to leave Montferrand in return for an indemnity.

In 1138 Zangī devised a plan to gain Ḥimṣ and establish a foothold in Damascus. A double marriage alliance was proposed to Shihāb al-Dīn Maḥmūd, namely that Zangī should marry the *atabeg*'s mother, Zumurrud Hatun, while Shihāb al-Dīn would marry Zangī's daughter. The two marriages, first agreed in May 1138, were concluded on 8 September, and Zangī received the city and citadel of Ḥimṣ as his wife's dowry. Beyond this however his plan miscarried. He had hoped that Zumurrud Hatun would rule Damascus as his regent, but when he found his hopes unrealised he abandoned her.

This was not the end of the story. On 23 June 1139 Shihāb al-Dīn was murdered by three members of his household. Damascus seemed likely to slide into anarchy but was saved by the strong hand of the city's governor, Mu'īn al-Dīn Unur. He installed Shihāb al-Dīn's half-brother, Jamāl al-Dīn Muḥammad, as the new *atabeg*, whereupon Zumurrud Hatun in an angry and vengeful spirit called upon Zangī for help. On his way southwards Zangī made a diversion to besiege Ba'labakk, which surrendered in October, and was granted to Najm al-Dīn Ayyūb. In December 1139 Zangī reached Damascus. He did not attempt a siege, still less a direct attack. Meanwhile Jamāl al-Dīn fell ill. He died on 29 March 1140, and Unur again took charge as the *atabeg* of Jamāl al-Dīn's young son and successor, Mujīr al-Dīn Uvak.

An interesting move had been made in 1139. Needing support against Zangī, Unur turned to the kingdom of Jerusalem, which, as he pointed out, would be seriously threatened if Zangī added Damascus to his holdings of Mosul and Aleppo. He offered to give the Franks Bāniyās at the southern foot of Mount Hermon, which however would first have to be taken from one of Zangī's retainers. This was duly accomplished. In June 1140 Zangī reappeared outside Damascus, but he could no longer count on an easy victory. The problem was solved, at least superficially, when Mujīr al-Dīn Uvak offered Zangī formal recognition as suzerain by the inclusion of his name in the *khuṭba*.

Over the next four years Zangī had little to do with events in Syria. Relations became extremely strained with Sultan Mas'ūd, who planned to attack Zangī in 1143–4. The matter was finally smoothed over, and Zangī received the sultan's command to attack Edessa. Since 1131 the county had been ruled by Joscelin II. As the north-eastern bastion of the Frankish states, Edessa occupied a curious geographical position. Half of it, including the capital city, lay east of the Euphrates, and hence far eastward of the other Frankish states, confined as they were to the coast and immediate hinterland of Syria-Palestine. As we have seen, the city had been held previously by the Armenians as successors to the Byzantines, and a numerous Armenian population continued to dwell there side by side with the Syrians and the Franks. West of the Euphrates, a virtual second capital was constituted by the stronghold and town of Turbessel.

At the beginning of August 1144 the Artukid lord of Ḥiṣn Kayfā (now Hasankeyf) and Khartpert died and was succeeded by his son, Kara Arslan. At the time Zangī was operating in this region as a prelude to a frontal attack on the city of Edessa. Kara Arslan sought support from Joscelin, and in response the count sent a raiding force to al-Raqqa. As Zangī took no action over this, Joscelin felt that it was safe for him to leave Edessa for his western territories. Warned of this, Zangī launched his attack on the city, and joined his forces there on 28 November 1144. In Joscelin's absence the defence was led by Hugh, the Frankish Catholic archbishop. No help came from Antioch. John Comnenus and King Fulk of Jerusalem had both been killed in hunting accidents in 1143, and neither of their successors, Manuel Comnenus and Queen Melisende, intervened in this crisis. After a siege of some four weeks the walls were breached, and the city fell on Christmas Eve of 1144. A massacre ensued but was stopped by Zangī, who restored the local authorities and installed a Muslim garrison in the citadel. Zangī remained in the neighbourhood, taking Sarūj and besieging al-Bīra (now Birecik) on the eastern bank of the Euphrates until events caused his return to Mosul in May 1145.

The sequel to the fall of Edessa: the Second Crusade

In the years following the fall of Edessa the significance of what had happened became increasingly clear. At first the loss seemed recoverable by action locally. Joscelin II still held the western half of his county containing his headquarters at Turbessel and other strongholds, as well as the bridgehead of al-Bīra. In October and November 1146 he succeeded in regaining and briefly holding the city of Edessa, but this was to be of no lasting significance.

Zangī had already passed from the scene. He was murdered by his own *mamlūk*s on the night of 14–15 September 1146, and his dominions were thereupon partitioned between two of his sons, the elder, Sayf al-Dīn Ghāzī, taking Mosul, and the second, Nūr al-Dīn Maḥmūd then aged 29, inheriting Aleppo.

Nūr al-Dīn was thus involved from the first with the problems of the Frankish–Muslim borderlands, and quickly showed his determination in dealing with Edessa. The Muslim garrison held out in the citadel, while the town was held by Joscelin. Nūr al-Dīn laid siege to Edessa, provisions ran scarce, and a sortie by Joscelin was massacred. The count himself escaped, and continued to hold his western territories until 1150, when he was captured by some Turcoman troops. He was sent to Aleppo, where he died a prisoner in 1159. His widow sold Turbessel and other strongholds to Manuel Comnenus, but within a year they had passed under Muslim rule.

More significant than Joscelin's brief reoccupation of Edessa was the response that the loss of the city provoked in Western Europe. This response ultimately took form in the Second Crusade, the leading propagandist for which was the Cistercian abbot, Bernard of Clairvaux. In this, as in other respects, the organisation of the Crusade was a matter of European politics and history, and had little bearing on the relations of the Frankish states with the Muslims until the Crusaders actually arrived in Syria-Palestine.

As the plans for the Crusade developed, it became essentially a co-operative venture of French and German military forces under Louis VII and Conrad III respectively. The Crusade was unwelcome to Manuel Comnenus on several grounds. After warfare with Antioch at the beginning of his reign, he had established good relations with Raymond who, as mentioned, renewed his oath of fealty to the Byzantine emperor in 1145. Two years later Manuel made peace with the Seljuks of Rūm in order to concentrate on danger from the Normans in Sicily. A Crusade, especially one under French leadership, might endanger his relationship with the Frankish states, where the rulers and nobility were predominantly of French extraction. Relations with Germany, valued by Byzantium as a counterpoise to the Normans of Sicily, might be endangered, although here Manuel had some security by virtue of his marriage to Conrad's sister-in-law. Generally, however, the emperor faced potential rather than immediate perils, which diplomacy and good fortune enabled him to avoid. He perforce welcomed the Crusade and gave it a measure of assistance, but by no means became as involved with it as Alexius Comnenus had been with the First Crusade. For their part, the Crusaders were resentful of Manuel's behaviour and that of the Byzantines generally, whom they deemed niggardly and extortionate in the matter of provisions. It was in these years that the anger that was to culminate in the seizure of Constantinople by the Fourth Crusade began to form.

The first of the two leaders of the Crusade to arrive in Syria was Louis VII, who was transported with some of his men from Attalia in Byzantine shipping. He reached Antioch in March 1148. Here as Raymond's guest he was given a plan of action for the Crusade. The recovery of Edessa should of course be its ultimate aim, but on the way the opportunity should be taken to attack Aleppo under its new lord, Nūr al-Dīn. In the following month Conrad arrived by sea, direct from Constantinople. He had fallen ill in Anatolia, had been cared for by Manuel personally, and then dispatched to Syria. He and Louis met at Tripoli, as the French king had announced his intention of making the pilgrimage to Jerusalem before starting military operations. The French and German troops were also mustering, although their numbers had been much reduced on the way. In Anatolia the Germans had been severely handled by the Rūm Seljuks at Dorylaeum, as they attempted the overland march to Syria. This was in October 1147, and in December they suffered another heavy defeat further south at Laodicea ad Lycum, near modern Denizli. For both the Germans and the French there then supervened the lack of enough shipping at Attalia to transport their diminished forces.

In June 1148 there was an event of decisive importance near Acre: a meeting of the High Court of the kingdom of Jerusalem and the leading Crusaders. Representatives of Antioch and Tripoli were not present, so a decision about the objective of the Crusade was taken entirely in the interest of the kingdom. Edessa seems to have dropped entirely out of the agenda, and it was decided to attack Damascus. This was a decision of dubious political wisdom in view of the special relationship between the kingdom and Damascus, which had originated, as already mentioned, when Mu'īn al-Dīn Unur, threatened by Zangī, concluded an alliance with King Fulk in 1139. With Zangī's death the immediate danger to Damascus had passed away, and indeed close friendly relations with Aleppo had been established, culminating in a marriage alliance with a daughter of Unur in March 1147. Thereafter Unur maintained a cautious pivotal position between Nūr al-Dīn and Jerusalem, playing off one against the other in order to secure his independence of both.

Their decision having been made, the Crusaders advanced by way of Bāniyās, and encamped on 24 July 1148 to the west of Damascus. On 27 July they moved to the more open ground east of the city, on the advice of their experienced comrades from Jerusalem, who realised the difficulty of delivering an attack through the orchards and gardens on the west. On 29 July they ended the short siege and withdrew their forces. Unur had called on Nūr al-Dīn and Ghāzī for help, and it was probably news of the advance of a relieving army that precipitated the Crusaders' withdrawal. For his part, Unur probably welcomed this outcome, since it saved him from having to admit such powerful and dangerous allies into the city, which would have ended the precarious diplomatic balance he had maintained since 1139. A further reason for the Crusaders' withdrawal was a rift between the nobles of Jerusalem, who wished to incorporate Damascus in the kingdom, and Count Thierry of Flanders, a leading Crusader, who hoped to become the ruler of Damascus as a new Frankish state.

This anticlimax outside Damascus was virtually the end of the Second Crusade. There was talk of an expedition to attack Ascalon, but nothing came of it. Conrad III left from Acre in September 1148. Louis VII stayed until after Easter 1149. When he returned to France, the idea of a new Crusade was mooted, chiefly among the clergy. But the French barons lacked enthusiasm for renewing their efforts so soon, and nothing resulted.

Runciman gives the title of 'The Turn of the Tide' to the part of his *History of the Crusades* that deals with life and events in the Frankish states after 1148. He opens with the words:

> The failure of the Second Crusade marks a turning-point in the story of Outremer. The fall of Edessa completed the first stage in the renascence of Islam; and the gains of Islam were confirmed by the pitiful collapse of the great expedition that was to have restored Frankish supremacy.[2]

But do the title and these words, reflecting as they do a modern retrospective view of the years following 1149, truly correspond to the Frankish or indeed to the Muslim assumptions of the time? The Second Crusade itself developed an ambiguity of aim as it proceeded. What began as an expedition to regain Edessa ended as an attempt to acquire new territory by the conquest of Damascus. In both respects the Crusade failed, but it is important to note that in its original aim the expedition prefigured the series of subsequent Crusades intended as wars of reconquest, while in the second aim it resumed the hope of the First Crusaders to extend the bounds of Christendom. This hope persisted during the ensuing decades, and the consequences were played out during the reign of Nūr al-Dīn as he vied with the Franks, especially the rulers of Jerusalem, for the control of Damascus and then of Egypt.

Notes

1. Peters, *First Crusade*, pp. 220–1.
2. Steven Runciman, *A History of the Crusades*, vol. II: *The Kingdom of Jerusalem*, Harmondsworth: Penguin, 1951, p. 291.

chapter four

NŪR AL-DĪN, SALADIN AND THE FRANKISH STATES

The reign of Nūr al-Dīn and the acquisition of Damascus

During his long reign from 1146 to his death in 1174, Nūr al-Dīn outlived all those who were his fellow rulers at his accession. In particular, his elder brother Ghāzī I, the *atabeg* of Mosul, died in November 1149, and thereby Nūr al-Dīn became the head of the Zangid clan. Ghāzī was succeeded by his son, Quṭb al-Dīn Mawdūd, and he by his son, Ghāzī II, in 1170. The history of Mosul was almost entirely distinct in this period from that of Nūr al-Dīn's possessions.

From the start Nūr al-Dīn was involved in dealings with the Frankish states on his borders. Apart from establishing his control over Edessa, and ultimately over the whole of the former county after Joscelin II's death as his prisoner in 1150, his first intervention was over a curious episode in 1148 in the county of Tripoli. Raymond II, the reigning count, was challenged by a pretender who had ensconced himself in the stronghold of ʻUrayma, an important strategic site dominating the coastal route near Latakia. Raymond called on Unur of Damascus for help, and then invited the cooperation of Nūr al-Dīn. Their success was complete, and the stronghold was demolished. The incident shows the Muslim powers in an unusual light as the chosen arbitrators in a purely Frankish concern, a reflection of their enhanced status after the Second Crusade.

Nūr al-Dīn's second involvement with the Franks came when he was asked by the reigning Seljuk sultan, Masʻūd, to intervene against Raymond of Antioch, who was raiding beyond the northern borders of his principality to the east of the Amanus mountains. The expedition was disastrous. Nūr al-Dīn was taken by surprise in his camp in November 1148, and was forced to flee to Aleppo. In the following year he took his revenge. In the summer of 1149 he planned to take Afāmiya on the middle Orontes, which had been captured by Tancred in 1106, and he called on Unur to provide a supporting contingent. Unur safeguarded himself by a two-year truce with Baldwin III in Muḥarram 544/May–June 1149, and then sent the required force. It was a second Field of Blood. Raymond was defeated and killed in the battle. Afāmiya was taken in July and Antioch itself besieged. In the meantime King Baldwin III brought in a relieving army and negotiated peace with Nūr al-Dīn. Apart from Afāmiya, Nūr al-Dīn failed at this time to advance his frontier to the Orontes. The stronghold of Ḥārim to the north was also taken, although not yet permanently held. It was to mark the effective frontier between Aleppo on the east and the Franks on the west. Antioch meanwhile remained, at least in name, under the rule of the Princess Constance, Raymond's widow.

While the political separation of Mosul and Aleppo simplified Nūr al-Dīn's tasks, since it allowed him to concentrate upon the problems of Muslim Syria, his position was weakened by the independent position of Damascus. Its *atabeg* at this time was the Burid Mujīr al-Dīn Uvak, Tuğtigin's great-grandson, but its real ruler until his death in August 1149 was the warlord Muʿīn al-Dīn Unur. His alliance with Jerusalem had thwarted Zangī's attempt to capture Damascus in 1140, and placed it in a precarious pivotal position between its Muslim and its Christian neighbour.

Nūr al-Dīn continued his father's policy towards Damascus, and sought to turn into reality the nominal suzerainty which, it will be remembered, had been formally conceded to Zangī in 1140. His opportunity came after Unur's death. Concealing the object of his expedition by declaring his intention of waging the *jihād* to protect the Ḥawrān against the Franks, he called upon the *atabeg* of Damascus to support him with a contingent of a thousand horsemen, and reproached the authorities for their alliance with the Franks. His demand was peremptorily rejected; in the Damascene chronicler's words, 'Between us and thee is nought but the sword, and a company of Franks is even now on the way to repel thee, shouldst thou advance upon us and beleaguer us'.[1] In fact it did not come to the sword. Peace was negotiated between Nūr al-Dīn and the Damascene authorities. Nūr al-Dīn, says the chronicler, 'was loth to shed the blood of the Muslims' and was also moved by 'certain reports' – presumably of Frankish intervention according to Unur's treaty with Baldwin III, which was not due to lapse until Muḥarram 546/April–May 1151. However that may be, the assertion of Nūr al-Dīn's suzerainty was solemnly confirmed by the mention of his name in the *khuṭba*, and ceremonially demonstrated by his grant of a robe of honour to Uvak. Henceforth he would wear the livery of his overlord, who thereupon returned to Aleppo in mid-May 1150.

Inside the city of Damascus conditions deteriorated. Uvak had little authority or popularity – there had in fact been a rising immediately after his accession, although it was quickly suppressed. In the very month when the agreement with Jerusalem expired, Nūr al-Dīn descended on Damascus, again calling on the authorities for cooperation in the *jihād*. Instead they again sought help from Jerusalem, although the chronicler says that 'all believing and right-minded men were filled with distress of mind and increasing aversion to such a hateful and repulsive state of affairs'.[2] As Baldwin III approached, Nūr al-Dīn withdrew into the mountains of Anti-Lebanon. The relieving force was inadequate to follow him, and set out instead on an expedition to bring Buṣrā back into obedience to Damascus. On the way it suffered a Turcoman attack, and withdrew to Jerusalem in early July 1151. About the same time Nūr al-Dīn resumed his siege of Damascus. It made no progress, and on 27 July peace was again negotiated. In the following October Uvak made a state visit to Nūr al-Dīn, who had in the meantime brought Buṣrā under his control. Uvak, we are told, 'promised allegiance to him and to act loyally as his agent in Damascus'.[3]

A deep rift was however opening between Uvak and his faction on the one hand, who were not averse to becoming a protectorate of Jerusalem, and on the other hand the people of Damascus, who preferred the domination of Nūr al-Dīn, not least because the Franks had imposed a heavy tribute and had acted arrogantly towards the Damascenes. A particular issue was that of the Christian slaves and captives in Damascus, which is thus described by Ibn al-Athīr:

> The Franks sent to review those male and female slaves of their people who had been taken from all the Christian lands, and bade them choose whether they would stay with their lords or return to their homelands. Anyone who preferred to stay was left, and anyone who wanted to go home went there.[4]

Meanwhile Nūr al-Dīn was playing on Uvak's fears to eliminate opponents among the Damascene leaders, while secretly building up support among his own partisans. In April 1154 he prepared to strike by sending his Kurdish army chief Shīrkūh, Saladin's uncle, with a force of a thousand men to Damascus. Uvak appealed to the Franks for help, but this was forestalled by Nūr al-Dīn, who joined Shīrkūh. Fighting began outside the city on 18 April. A week later Nūr al-Dīn's troops succeeded in finding an entry, whereupon Uvak took refuge in the citadel. Negotiations ensued, and Nūr al-Dīn entered the citadel on 25 April, the day that the city was taken. Uvak was granted assignments in Ḥimṣ for himself and his troops, but lost this compensation when he tried to stir up revolt in

Damascus. He fled to Baghdad, where he died in 1169. Nūr al-Dīn appointed Shīrkūh as his governor and representative in Damascus.

Although Nūr al-Dīn had now established his supremacy over the whole of Muslim Syria, the situation was far from stable. In particular he confronted the kingdom of Jerusalem, where also the state of affairs had recently and significantly changed. Although Baldwin III had nominally been king since the death of his father, Fulk of Anjou, in 1143, he was still a boy at the time, and his mother, Queen Melisende, assumed the regency. As he grew up, hostility developed between mother and son, and from 1149 they and their respective partisans split the kingdom. A scheme for its partition was drawn up in 1152 and rapidly collapsed. Civil warfare ensued. It ended with Baldwin's victory and the exclusion of Melisende from any part in the government.

During the decade following Nūr al-Dīn's annexation of Damascus, the relations between his realm and the kingdom of Jerusalem were characterised by alternating periods of truce and hostilities over the control of border strongholds. After gaining Damascus, Nūr al-Dīn at first moved cautiously. He continued the payment of tribute to Jerusalem that Unur had initiated, and in May 1155 he renewed for a year the treaty with Baldwin III. He rejected a proposal by Ṭalā'i' b. Ruzzīk, the Fatimid *wazīr* who was the actual ruler of Egypt, for joint action against Jerusalem, and he again renewed the truce with the kingdom towards the end of 1156.

This scene of harmony was abruptly shattered in February 1157, when Baldwin raided some Turcoman nomads who were pasturing Damascene horses and herds at the foot of Mount Hermon. This district was covered by treaty, and Nūr al-Dīn reacted vigorously to the raid, aiming to capture the Frankish stronghold of Bāniyās, which dominated the region. In May 1157 he took Bāniyās after a siege, but Baldwin III brought up a relieving force, which was able to retake the stronghold in June. He then withdrew, only to be ambushed and put to flight by Nūr al-Dīn at Jacob's Ford on the Jordan. Nūr al-Dīn again laid siege to Bāniyās, and again Baldwin prepared an expedition. This time he was supported by troops from Tripoli and Antioch. The latter were led by Reynald of Châtillon, a landless adventurer and a handsome knight, who in 1153 had married the widowed Princess Constance of Antioch. He was to prove the stormy petrel of the Latin East. On hearing of Baldwin's augmented forces, Nūr al-Dīn raised the siege of Bāniyās and returned to Damascus in August 1157.

Earthquakes severely affected the central Orontes region in the summer of 1157, and the Franks saw in this calamity a chance to strengthen their frontier against Nūr al-Dīn, who in fact suffered a serious illness followed by a long convalescence from October of the same year. Baldwin III joined forces with Reynald of Antioch, Raymond III of Tripoli and Count Thierry of Flanders, who had arrived on pilgrimage with a body of troops. They marched on Chastel Ruge, identified as ʿAllārūz lying east of the Orontes on the way to Maʿarrat al-Nuʿmān. They besieged the stronghold, but broke off the siege on hearing of the approach of Nūr al-Dīn's forces. Instead they turned against Shayzar, which occupied a strong position on the river itself. The city and its citadel had been devastated by an earthquake in August 1157, and Banū Munqidh, its Arab ruling family, was virtually exterminated. While the city itself was captured without much difficulty, the citadel, poised above, offered a more serious problem. At this point Thierry and Reynald quarrelled, and Baldwin was compelled to raise the siege. After Nūr al-Dīn had recovered his health, he visited Shayzar and refurbished its defences. Disappointed in their attempts to gain Chastel Ruge and Shayzar, the Frankish allies decided to make a last expedition against the border strongholds before Nūr al-Dīn's recovery. On this occasion they struck further north, and in December 1157 began the siege of Ḥārim (Harenc of the Franks, who had held it until 1149). It fell in February 1158 and was restored to its former lordship, the principality of Antioch. Thereupon the Frankish alliance broke up.

In the ensuing summer Nūr al-Dīn, restored to health, resumed the offensive with an expedition against Ḥabīs Jaldak, which was essentially a fortified cave lying east of the Jordan and south of the Yarmūk. It was thus a stronghold threatening the south-western approaches to Damascus. Nūr al-Dīn set out in May 1158 but, hearing that Baldwin and Thierry were bringing up a relieving force, he broke off the siege and retreated towards Damascus. On the way he was intercepted and heavily defeated by the Franks. A de facto truce with Baldwin followed. The next year saw inconclusive warfare and the renewal of truces. In 1161 the situation was sufficiently stable to allow Nūr al-Dīn to make the pilgrimage to Mecca, confirming his reputation as a pious Muslim. His attempt to regain Harenc in 1162 ended in negotiations. In February 1163 Baldwin III died childless, and the crown of Jerusalem passed to his brother Amalric.

In the meantime the attitude of Byzantium towards the Frankish states was changing as a policy of détente came into being under Manuel Comnenus. As has been mentioned, Raymond of Antioch fell in the battle of Inab in 1149, and for a while it seemed that the widowed Princess Constance might accept a Byzantine suitor as her second husband. But his proposal was rejected and, as we have seen, she married the adventurer Reynald of Châtillon. Between 1152 and 1158 Manuel was preoccupied in the Balkans and with Norman Italy. By this time the weakness of the Frankish states before Nūr al-Dīn was becoming apparent, and in 1157 Baldwin III turned to Manuel and sent a delegation to obtain a Byzantine princess in marriage. The negotiations were protracted but succeeded in the end, and in 1158 Baldwin married Theodora Comnena, a niece of the emperor.

Antioch and its prince had been in a sense bypassed and isolated by this alliance between Byzantium and Jerusalem. This was made very clear later in the year when Manuel led out his army, ultimately intended for an attack on Antioch. He reconquered the plain of Cilicia from the Armenians and wintered at Misis. Reynald, deeply compromised by a joint raid with the Armenians on Byzantine Cyprus in 1156, hastened to the emperor's camp to make a most humble and public submission, and to appeal for mercy. There he swore fealty to Manuel and undertook to surrender the citadel of Antioch to him. Baldwin, arriving shortly afterwards, was honourably received and established himself on good terms with the emperor. In April 1159 Manuel made a splendid triumphal state entry into Antioch. His vassal, Prince Reynald, accompanied him on foot as his stirrup-holder, and his ally, King Baldwin, rode behind him, though without any royal insignia. After a week of feasts Manuel withdrew to his camp outside the city. The significance of events was clear; there had been a revolution in Byzantine policy. The annexation of the lands into which the Crusaders had intruded was no longer sought; instead they were symbolically reunited to the Empire and became in theory a protectorate.

The political and military fruits of the new relationship appeared when the state entry of April 1159 was followed by a joint expedition of the Byzantines under Manuel and the Franks led by Baldwin and Reynald against Nūr al-Dīn. The two armies met on the river 'Afrīn, a northern tributary of the Orontes, but negotiations took the place of fighting. In May a truce was arranged, which Nūr al-Dīn secured by the release of thousands of Christian prisoners, many of them taken during the Second Crusade. Thereafter the allies dispersed. In 1160 Baldwin, Reynald and the Armenians sent supporting troops to Manuel for a campaign that he waged successfully against Kılıc Arslan II, the Seljuk sultan of Rūm.

Between 1161 and 1163 there were several shifts in the kaleidoscope of power. Reynald of Antioch was captured in a skirmish in 1160 or 1161, and began a 16-year imprisonment in Aleppo. A further tie between the principality and the Empire was established in 1161 when Manuel married Maria, the daughter of Princess Constance. After frequent clashes between Constance and the barons of Antioch her son, Bohemond III, was at last installed as ruler. Finally, as mentioned, Amalric succeeded

Baldwin as king of Jerusalem in February 1163. The new relationship between the kingdom and the Empire was again shown in 1167, when Amalric married another of Manuel's nieces, Maria Comnena.

The contest for Egypt

Although clashes over the border strongholds between Nūr al-Dīn and Amalric continued, their importance was overshadowed in the next six years by a struggle in quite another field – the contest for Egypt. The antecedents to this contest must first be briefly considered.

Held back from further expansion towards the east by the strength of Aleppo and Damascus, united since 1154 in the hand of Nūr al-Dīn, the authorities in Jerusalem began to show an interest in Egypt, where a growing propensity to anarchic factionalism was cloaked by the empty form of the Fatimid caliphate. The first steps were taken by Baldwin III, who by 1150 had refortified the ancient site of Gaza, and thereby isolated Ascalon, the last Fatimid garrison in Palestine. Operations against Ascalon itself began in 1153. The city surrendered in August, and in the following year Baldwin bestowed the combined fiefs of Jaffa and Ascalon on Amalric.

Meanwhile actual power in Egypt had passed in 1154 to the *wazīr* Ṭalā'i' b. Ruzzīk, who installed al-'Āḍid, then a child of nine, who was to be the last Fatimid caliph. Ṭalā'i' fell a victim to factional hostility in September 1161, and was succeeded as *wazīr* by his son, Ruzzīk. This touched off a contest over the wazirate, which gave the neighbours of Egypt in Syria-Palestine the opportunity for intervention. It may be noted that all the contenders for the wazirate were Arab magnates. Egypt had never formed part of the Seljuk Empire, and so had not experienced the Turkish domination of the ruling and military elites that had occurred in the other parts of the Near East. The powerful military factions in Egypt were Arab and Berber tribesmen who had come in from the Maghrib with the ruling dynasty, and also black slave-troops (*Sūdān*), obtained from or through Nubia, the region above the First Cataract of the Nile.

The struggle for the wazirate began with an armed confrontation in 1162 between Ruzzīk and Shāwar, the governor of Upper Egypt, who came from a partially settled beduin tribe. Shāwar was successful; Ruzzīk was captured and was put to death in the following year. But Shāwar, now *wazīr* and commander-in-chief (*amīr al-juyūsh*), was forthwith confronted by another contender, the military chief Ḍirghām, an Arab and perhaps a descendant of pre-Islamic kings. He raised a revolt in August 1163 on the pretext of avenging Ruzzīk, and superseded Shāwar as *wazīr* in September. Shāwar fled, and made his way to Nūr al-Dīn in Damascus by October 1163.

Meanwhile the Franks were increasing their intervention in Egypt. Amalric had been sent by Baldwin III on an expedition against Egypt in 1163, and had been appeased by a promise of Egyptian tribute. Once he had become king in 1163, he made a demand for the payment of this tribute the pretext for an expedition, and in September penetrated the eastern edge of the Nile Delta to within some 48 km of Cairo. The Egyptian army, headed by a brother of Ḍirghām, fell back on Bilbays, and an order was given to cut the defences that secured Egypt against the Nile flood. Amalric retreated and his expedition failed.

Shāwar made huge promises to Nūr al-Dīn if he would give him military help to regain his post. Above all he undertook to accept Nūr al-Dīn as his overlord, and to allow a Syrian expeditionary force to act only in accordance with orders from Damascus. Here another factor enters the equation. The Syrian force would be under the command of Shīrkūh, and the Kurdish amir was by no means a passive observer of events. He had played an important part in Nūr al-Dīn's rise to ascendancy in Syria: he commanded his forces and became his principal adviser. As such, he had a large share in persuading Nūr al-Dīn to intervene in Egypt. Ḍirghām also made overtures seeking Nūr al-Dīn's support, but as these failed he turned to Amalric, promising to pay tribute if he were given help. In this way the struggle over the wazirate escalated into a potential conflict between Amalric and Nūr al-Dīn. Both parties recognised the danger, and both were anxious to limit the area of possible conflict.

Shīrkūh however, possibly with the hope of rendering himself independent, overcame Nūr al-Dīn's hesitation, and in April 1164 led a Syrian force into Egypt to reinstate Shāwar. Ḍirghām sent a panic-stricken cry for help to Amalric, offering a treaty of alliance that would have subordinated Egypt to the kingdom of Jerusalem. Amalric was willing to intervene, but was anticipated by Shīrkūh, who laid Cairo under siege in May. Ḍirghām lost the support of the people, the troops and the caliph, and was killed when attempting to flee on 24 May. Shāwar was restored as *wazīr*, but refused to pay the promised tribute to Nūr al-Dīn.

The elimination of Ḍirghām had led Amalric to withhold his intervention in Egypt, but now his aid was sought by Shāwar. The army of Jerusalem, reinforced by pilgrim warriors, mustered at Ascalon, and towards the beginning of July 1164 it set out on a second invasion of Egypt. Once again the immediate objective was the eastern edge of the Delta, where Shīrkūh and his nephew Saladin (Ṣalāḥ al-Dīn b. Ayyūb) awaited them in Bilbays. There the Muslims were besieged from August to October 1164 by the Franks, aided by Shāwar with the Fatimid forces. After prolonged and devious negotiations involving Amalric, Shīrkūh and Shāwar, the king and the Syrian commander ended the deadlock by mutually agreeing to withdraw from Egypt. Amalric had been driven to this by his growing anxiety for the security of the kingdom. Nūr al-Dīn had waged a campaign during his absence that had led to the taking of Ḥārim in August 1164 and Bāniyās in October. Shīrkūh for his part was conscious of the hardships suffered by his troops during the long siege of Bilbays, and was anxious to end the deadlock. By November 1164 Egypt was cleared of both invaders, and under the rule of Shāwar as *wazīr*.

Shīrkūh's ambition to control Egypt had now been thoroughly roused, and over the next couple of years he pressed his demands for a second invasion on the cautious and reluctant Nūr al-Dīn. In a sense he bypassed his master by a direct appeal to al-Mustanjid, the ʻAbbasid caliph, to sanction operations against the Fatimid anti-caliphate in Cairo. This invocation of the caliph set a precedent that Saladin was later to follow. At last as 1167 approached, Nūr al-Dīn gave his consent to an expedition. When news of this reached Jerusalem, preparations began for a counter-invasion. Shāwar resumed his previous good relations with Amalric, and their agreement was confirmed in an audience that the Caliph al-ʻĀḍiḍ granted to the Frankish envoys.

The two forces left for Egypt about the same time, early in the year 1167, but their major confrontation did not occur until 18 March, when a pitched battle took place at al-Bābayn, south of Ashmunayn in Middle Egypt. The result was indecisive but Shīrkūh moved to take control of Alexandria, which the combined Franks and Egyptians besieged for three months. During the siege Shīrkūh escaped, leaving Saladin as governor of the city. Once again Amalric and Shīrkūh found matters at a deadlock. Neither was strong enough for a decisive victory. Amalric was again anxious about Syria, where Nūr al-Dīn had occupied Ḥūnīn, the Frankish Castel Neuf, near Bāniyās. Shīrkūh was alarmed at Saladin's dangerous situation in Alexandria. In these circumstances it was not difficult for the two contenders to come to an agreement which, as in 1164, was based upon a joint withdrawal of their forces. This took place in August 1167, but Amalric left a Frankish representative in Cairo to ensure the payment of the annual Egyptian tribute.

The matter of Egypt remained to be resolved. A new turn was given to events by the marriage, mentioned earlier, of Amalric to the Byzantine princess, Maria Comnena. This took place on 29 August 1167, shortly after the Frankish withdrawal from Egypt. A joint expedition against Egypt was certainly discussed with the Byzantine envoys at the time of the wedding, but Amalric anticipated this when, in October 1168, he led out his forces from Ascalon on the well-known route to the eastern Delta and Cairo. Bilbays was taken at the beginning of November after a siege of three days. The Franks advanced to besiege Cairo, while Shāwar evacuated and set fire to the ancient city of al-Fusṭāṭ. At this point al-ʿĀḍiḍ sent an appeal for help to Nūr al-Dīn: it is not clear how far this was on Shāwar's initiative. The appeal was answered, and in mid-December Shīrkūh set out again, this time as the expected liberator of Egypt from the Franks. Amalric realised his inability to withstand Shīrkūh, and on 2 January 1169 began the retreat to Palestine. Six days later the Syrian expeditionary force reached Cairo. Nūr al-Dīn had conceded full powers to Shīrkūh in regard to his army. He was furthermore appointed *wazīr* by al-ʿĀḍiḍ when Shāwar was murdered (on Shīrkūh's order) on 13 January 1169. As such he became the effective ruler of Egypt. His wazirate was short. He died on 23 March 1169, and three days later Saladin accepted al-ʿĀḍiḍ's commission to succeed his uncle. The contest for Cairo had ended. The land of Egypt with its immense resources had been annexed to Nūr al-Dīn's Syrian realm and was at Saladin's disposal.

The extension of Saladin's power: 1169–86

From the time of Saladin's succession to the command of the Syrian expeditionary force and his concurrent appointment as al-ʿĀḍiḍ's *wazīr*, two phases are distinguishable in his career. The second and much shorter phase in the year 1187 consisted of his victorious *jihād*, the crowning mercy of Ḥaṭṭīn, the liberation of Jerusalem and the almost complete recovery of the Palestinian coastline from the Franks.

In the earlier and far longer phase, by contrast, Saladin was chiefly concerned with establishing his hold over Egypt and, after Nūr al-Dīn's death in May 1174, over his former master's possessions in Muslim Syria also. As far as Egypt was concerned, he faced some dangers from the outset, and these were linked to a considerable extent with anomalies in his own position as being at one and the same time the viceroy of a pious Sunni ruler and the *wazīr* of a Shiʿi Fatimid caliph.

His first problem was to constitute a reliable military force under his own control. Shīrkūh's death and Saladin's succession to the command had opened up a distinction in the expeditionary force between the Nūriyya, the contingent directly dependent on Nūr al-Dīn, and the Asadiyya, the troops personally levied by Asad al-Dīn Shīrkūh. One of the leading Syrian generals decided that he had no future in Saladin's

Egypt, and made his way back to Damascus. To compensate for such weaknesses Saladin formed his own guards regiment, the Ṣalāḥiyya, and encouraged members of his own family to migrate to Egypt. An important recruit in July 1169 was his brother Tūrān-Shāh, who was to play a significant part in military operations. Other immigrants included his two nephews, Taqī al-Dīn ʻUmar and Farrukh-Shāh. Saladin's old father, Ayyūb, arrived in April 1170. The hold on Egypt of the family, and thus of Saladin himself, was strengthened by the grant of important financial assignments (*iqṭāʻs*). Ayyūb received Alexandria, Damietta and al-Buḥayra, i.e. the two principal Mediterranean ports and the western frontier province. Tūrān-Shāh was granted the provinces of Upper Egypt, Qūs, Aswān and the Red Sea port of ʻAydhāb – places that were difficult to control as they were remote from the centre of power in Cairo.

By bringing in his own kinsmen and using his extended family as a basis of security for his power in Egypt, Saladin had produced a political structure that perhaps reflected his own marginality. As a Kurd he belonged to neither of the two ruling groups in the Near East, the Turks and the Arabs. As Nūr al-Dīn's lieutenant, he was the vassal of a Turkish lord; as al-ʻĀḍiḍ's *wazīr*, he was the minister of an Arab caliph. By the importation of his family to strengthen his hand, he foreshadowed the future development of the Ayyubid realm as a clan confederacy. In Egypt the Ayyubid period was a Kurdish intermezzo, linking the Arab Fatimid past and the Turkish Mamluk future.

Meanwhile Saladin had to face and surmount an internal and external threat. The internal threat came from the palace, the headquarters of the Fatimid caliphate and its administration, which lived on uneasy terms with the new military masters of the country. In August 1169 a principal contingent of the palace's armed forces, the black troops, rose in the centre of Cairo, and advanced on the *wazīr*'s residence. Resistance to them was led by Tūrān-Shāh and supported by troops of the Ṣalāḥiyya. Al-ʻĀḍiḍ looked on at the conflict but did not intervene on the black troops' behalf, and they were driven down to the Zuwayla Gate at the southern end of the city. They asked for quarter, and were allowed to cross the Nile to Giza. They were followed there by Tūrān-Shāh, and massacred on 23 August.

The external threat came from the Franks. King Amalric was preparing yet another attack on Egypt, and was supported on this occasion by an embarassingly large Byzantine naval squadron from Manuel Comnenus. The two forces descended on Damietta, which was laid under siege in October 1169. The siege dragged on until the middle of December, when the allies withdrew on thoroughly bad terms with each other. Saladin celebrated his twofold success over internal and external enemies, and followed this up with an offensive against the Franks in 1170. Making a feint against southern Palestine he captured and briefly held Gaza on 13 December, while his main objective, the fortress of Ayla at the head of the gulf of ʿAqaba, fell to a joint land and naval attack at the end of the year. Saladin returned victorious from this *jihād* in February 1171.

Saladin's growing fame and independence were by no means wholly congenial to Nūr al-Dīn, who from the outset seems to have been somewhat jealous of his viceroy. However in 1171, on Nūr al-Dīn's initiative, Saladin took a step that accorded with his master's piety and his own, and at the same time removed a basic anomaly of his position in Egypt. This was the ending of the Shiʿi Fatimid caliphate and the return of Egypt to the majority of Muslim states that recognised the nominal supremacy of the Sunni ʿAbbasid caliphate of Baghdad. Saladin had long been taking steps to enhance Sunni influence and authority at official levels. He now sought the agreement of his supporters for the final move. It was taken in two stages. On the first Friday in AH 567 (10 September 1171) the name of the Fatimid caliph was omitted from the *khuṭba*, and in one mosque the ʿAbbasid caliph, al-Mustaḍīʾ, was specifically mentioned in his place. This was in effect a trying of the water, in which Saladin did not take a prominent part. Meanwhile al-ʿĀḍiḍ lay dying in his palace. He expired on the night of 12–13 September, having learnt that his name had been omitted from the *khuṭba*. On the following Friday, 17 September, the *khuṭba* was pronounced in the name of the Caliph al-Mustaḍīʾ without occasioning any overt protests. Saladin then confined the remaining members of the Fatimid family under house arrest, and brought the succession to an end.

Signs of tension between Nūr al-Dīn and Saladin continued to appear during the three remaining years of their partnership in power. This was basically because Nūr al-Dīn's attention was centred upon Syria and Saladin's upon Egypt. In practice the stress showed itself in two matters: finance and military cooperation. The fabled wealth of Egypt and the rumoured treasure of the Fatimid palace had produced a popular expectation that when these were exploited all the difficulties of the Near East would be solved. In fact the exploitation of these resources, such as they were, was carried out by Saladin in his own interests. Nothing was sent to Nūr al-Dīn before 1172, and thereafter he received only a meagre tribute from Saladin. Apart from curios and precious objects, Saladin dispatched 100,000 dinars in specie in April 1172 and a further 60,000 dinars in May 1173. Finally, early in 1174, Nūr al-Dīn sent one of his chief officials to carry out an audit of the state finances of Egypt. Saladin reacted angrily to this intrusion into his affairs, but in the end he agreed to cooperate. The situation changed when Nūr al-Dīn died after a short illness on 15 May 1174.

Nūr al-Dīn's hope that Saladin would cooperate with him in combined action against Jerusalem was also disappointed. Nūr al-Dīn chiefly wanted to secure communications between Egypt and Syria by capturing or otherwise containing the great Frankish strongholds in the east of the kingdom. Saladin's capture and destruction of Ayla in 1170 was indeed a contribution to this object. In 1171 a project for joint operations against al-Karak failed when Saladin, defeated in a conflict with nomad Arabs, broke off his advance and returned to Cairo. A further expedition by Saladin alone against al-Karak and al-Shawbak in the summer of 1173 ended prematurely, the death of Saladin's father being at least the pretext for this. There was no other action before Nūr al-Dīn's death in the following year.

In 1174 a curious coincidence occurred in the political situation of Nūr al-Dīn's realm and the kingdom of Jerusalem. Nūr al-Dīn died in May, leaving as his heir his only son, al-Ṣāliḥ Ismā'īl, 11 years of age. On 11 July King Amalric died, and was also succeeded by his only son, the 13-year-old Baldwin IV, who was a leper. The death of these two energetic rulers greatly enhanced Saladin's position, especially as regards al-Ṣāliḥ, who was safeguarded by no such automatic right of succession as was Baldwin, but was surrounded by guardians and advisers who were jealous of each other, of Saladin, and of the rulers of the other Zangid territories.

On 25 July 1174 al-Ṣāliḥ and the inner circle of his court moved to Aleppo, the capital of northern Syria with its great citadel. Saladin, who from the outset asserted his loyalty to al-Ṣāliḥ, entered Damascus on 28 October, meeting virtually no opposition. From this point his immediate concern was to strengthen and extend his hold over southern Syria. At the same time he inevitably inherited one of Nūr al-Dīn's major commitments – the *jihād* against the kingdom of Jerusalem. For the time being this was subordinated to other military activities designed to safeguard his personal position.

To the Zangids and their supporters Saladin necessarily appeared as a usurper. For his part he was concerned in the first place with the acquisition of Syrian territory, and in the second place with securing his own legitimacy in the face of Zangid hostility. It is not necessary to enter into the details of his campaigns and diplomacy in this period, but the developments must be briefly indicated. The maintenance of Damascus against the Zangids necessitated the securing of its northern approaches by the key points of Ḥimṣ and Ḥamāh. The town of Ḥimṣ was taken in December 1174, although its citadel held out until the following March.

Ḥamāh surrendered to Saladin in December 1174 also. An army from Mosul under the command of Mas'ūd, the brother and eventual successor of Ghāzī II, its Zangid lord, advanced on Saladin, and was defeated near Ḥamāh in April 1175. Subsequent negotiations left Saladin in possession of his conquests and also of Ma'arrat al-Nu'mān, a useful gain to the north between Ḥamāh and Aleppo. Another victory over the Zangids at Tall al-Sulṭān, south of Aleppo, in April 1176 was followed by the acquisition of strategically placed localities to the north and north-east of the city. A direct attack on Aleppo itself had failed at the end of 1174, and in 1176 Saladin's strategy clearly aimed at the encirclement of the city and the cutting of its lines of communications.

The next major development on this front came when al-Ṣāliḥ died in Aleppo in December 1181 at the age of 19. His kinsman Mas'ūd, now lord of Mosul, took charge of the city. The administration he set up proved unpopular, and early in 1182 it was decided that Aleppo should pass to his brother, Zangī II, the lord of Sinjār. Saladin's final push to gain Aleppo ensued. In September 1182 he was outside Aleppo, engaged in fruitless conversations with Zangī, but then he moved across the Euphrates to al-Bīra to attack Upper Mesopotamia. Edessa, al-Raqqa, the towns of the Khābūr valley, and Nuṣaybīn fell to him. A siege of Mosul itself in November failed, and Saladin had to content himself with taking Sinjār. After wintering at Nuṣaybīn, Saladin moved on Aleppo once again, and arrived outside the city on 21 May 1183. With his mobile fighting force he had shown himself able to match the Zangids in the heart of their possessions. Zangī was both ready and willing to return to Sinjār, and on 21 June 1183 Saladin at last entered the citadel of Aleppo. Nearly three years later the last piece of his jigsaw fell into place when, after a siege of Mosul and Saladin's own disablement by a serious illness, a peace treaty was made with Mas'ūd on 3 March 1186. The lord of Mosul recognised Saladin as his suzerain, and agreed to cooperate with him in military operations.

To assert the legitimacy of his position in these years, Saladin used two principal means. In the first place, he moved over the heads of his opponents by maintaining constant relations with the 'Abbasid caliph in Baghdad, the sole source of legitimate authority for Sunni rulers. After his occupation of Damascus he asked the Caliph al-Mustaḍī' to invest him not only with Egypt but also Syria, all the former possessions of Nūr al-Dīn and any future conquests. The caliph replied cautiously, investing Saladin only with the territories he already held. He sent Saladin robes of honour, thus visibly investing him with these limited territories, and at the same time he sent robes of honour to al-Ṣāliḥ, thereby recognising him as the legitimate heir of Nūr al-Dīn. In 1180 al-Mustaḍī' was succeeded by his vigorous son, the Caliph al-Nāṣir. When, after al-Ṣāliḥ's death in 1181, Mas'ūd of Mosul appeared as the protector of Aleppo, Saladin asked al-Nāṣir for investiture with Mosul and Upper Mesopotamia, but the caliph merely granted him permission to take Āmid. Saladin's attempts to obtain legitimacy by involving the caliph in his political scheming, although pertinacious, were largely circumvented.

Saladin also sought to prove himself the legitimate successor of Nūr al-Dīn by his prowess in the *jihād*. In this sphere of action his enterprises in the years from 1174 to 1186 were remarkably limited, and some of them were responses to pressure from Jerusalem under its young and still vigorous king, Baldwin the leper. In July 1176 the Franks were raiding close to Damascus and also in the Biqā'. Saladin's brother, Tūrān-Shāh, commanding the forces of Damascus, confronted them at 'Ayn al-Jarr and was heavily defeated. In November 1177 Saladin took the initiative by marching on Ascalon, but then allowed his troops to disperse in raids up the coast of Palestine. Baldwin led his army out of Ascalon, and encountered the Muslims at a site called Mount Gisard, probably not far from the city. Once again Saladin was defeated. A serious threat to Muslim communications was constituted when, in October, Baldwin started to build a fortress, Bayt al-Aḥzān, to control the crossing of the Jordan at Jacob's Ford. At first Saladin hoped to stop its construction by offering an indemnity to the Franks. When this gesture failed, he decided to take action, and captured Bayt al-Aḥzān in August 1179.

In the meantime an important battle had taken place with the Franks. Roused by frequent Muslim raids, Baldwin had led his army northwards from Tiberias to a point overlooking the Līṭānī river and the plain of Marj 'Uyūn on its western side. There the Franks were caught between the forces of Saladin and his nephew, Farrukh-Shāh, and were heavily defeated in June 1179. Baldwin himself escaped with difficulty. Truce was made between Saladin and the kingdom by the summer of 1180, but it did not prove durable. In July 1181 Saladin, working with Farrukh-Shāh, unsuccessfully attacked Baysān, was resisted by a Frankish force, and an inconclusive battle took place.

In the following years much of the conflict between Saladin and the kingdom of Jerusalem was centred in Oultrejourdain, the territory of Transjordan with the great castle of al-Karak, Le Crac of the Franks, west of the Dead Sea. At the time the lord of Oultrejourdain was Reynald of Châtillon, who had acquired the territory in right of his second wife, the heiress Stephanie. Reynald was, as has been seen, a violent adventurer, and, as in the past, he showed his propensity to ill-considered action. His territory was situated on the border of the Hijaz with its two Holy Cities of Mecca and Medina, and he planned a project of invading the region by land from al-Karak. About the middle of 1181 he advanced south-eastwards towards Tabūk on the route from Damascus to the Holy Cities. Farrukh-Shāh went to oppose him, and in December Reynald withdrew to his own territory. He had now a more ambitious scheme in mind. In the following winter he made a reconnaissance of the routes into Arabia, and also began to construct ships for naval operations. These were ready in 1183 and were transported to the gulf of ʻAqaba. The maritime attack he then delivered caused general alarm among Muslims. Hitherto the Red Sea had been closed to the Franks, but the expedition attacked the important port of ʻAydhāb on the Nubian coast, and then crossed to attack places on the coast of the Hijaz. The Frankish activities were checked by a naval force from Egypt. Its admiral caught and destroyed the Frankish ships, and the survivors of the raiders were beheaded in Mecca and Cairo.

Following these events Saladin made two attempts to take al-Karak itself. The first was made in November 1183. Saladin occupied the town that had grown up around the castle, and besieged the castle, where Reynald was celebrating the marriage of his stepson to the Princess Isabel, King Baldwin's sister. A Frankish relieving force was sent to the south of the Dead Sea, but Saladin did not attempt to challenge it, and withdrew early in December. The second attempt, made in the summer of 1184, was virtually a repetition of the first. Saladin moved to Oultrejourdain in July, and began the siege of the castle on 23 August. By the end of the month it seemed near to falling, but at this point a Frankish relieving force crossed the Jordan and Saladin broke off the siege and withdrew.

Saladin's *jihād* was now increasingly assuming the aspect of a personal duel with Reynald of Châtillon, a rivalry of two self-made men, both somewhat detached from the communities of which they were the champions. Saladin's dislike of Reynald was exacerbated by the latter's capture of an Egyptian caravan as it passed through Oultrejourdain with a military escort. When Reynald refused to release the prisoners, Saladin swore to kill him – an oath that he was soon to fulfil.

So far, in spite of Saladin's frequent evocations of the *jihād* as the motive of his actions, operations against the Franks had played a far less important part in his military activities than the campaigns by which he brought first Damascus, then Aleppo and finally Mosul under his supremacy, and united Muslim Syria under the control of himself and his family. He was now free to move to decisive action against the Franks, and to overthrow the kingdom of Jerusalem. Had this been his intention throughout, or had the *jihād* been mere propaganda to conceal and justify his power-politics?

Ḥaṭṭīn and the Third Crusade

The situation inside the kingdom also changed in these years to favour hostilities by Saladin. Baldwin IV the leper died in 1185, leaving as his next of kin his sister Sibyl and her infant son by her deceased first husband, who was crowned as Baldwin V. In 1180 Sibyl had remarried. Her second husband was Guy of Lusignan, a feckless youth and a newcomer to the Holy Land. When Baldwin V died in August 1186, Sibyl was crowned as queen of Jerusalem, and in turn she crowned her husband as king. Henceforward there was an open rift between a faction headed by Guy and another led by Count Raymond III of Tripoli, who had played a leading part under Baldwin IV.

So when Saladin mustered his forces for a frontal attack on the kingdom in May 1187, the Frankish forces were far from being of one mind. Raymond advocated a defensive strategy, but King Guy was easily persuaded otherwise. The decisive battle took place on 4 July near the village of Ḥaṭṭīn, north-west of Tiberias. The Franks were heavily defeated, and the prisoners included Guy himself and Reynald of Châtillon. The story of how Saladin spared the king but personally cut down his old rival and enemy is well known. More important than this incident was the destruction of the field army of Jerusalem. The whole kingdom lay open for Saladin to conquer, and he made an easy advance through the coastland.

Tyre alone was saved from capitulation by the unexpected arrival of a young Crusader, Conrad of Montferrat, who prepared to resist Saladin. The siege was raised and Saladin departed to besiege Ascalon, which surrendered on 4 September 1187 in exchange for the release of King Guy and his noble captives. Saladin went on to Jerusalem, where after a short siege he negotiated the surrender of the city and the evacuation of its Frankish inhabitants – an ironic contrast to its capture by the bloodthirsty Crusaders in 1099. Saladin entered Jerusalem on 2 October, and the elimination of all traces of the Frankish regime began forthwith. The golden cross was removed from the Dome of the Rock, as were the tokens of Christianity from all the sites sacred to Muslims. The Latin kingdom survived only in such of its coastal cities and fortresses as it could hold or regain. When, after the recovery of Jerusalem, Saladin sent his forces against Tyre, Conrad's tenacious defence withstood a siege from November until the end of the year. On New Year's Day 1188 Saladin broke off the siege and dispersed the forces that he had mustered for the *jihād* from Egypt, Syria and Mosul.

Meanwhile King Guy, whose authority had been flatly rejected by Conrad of Montferrat, had gathered together a fighting force and started his own campaign for the reconquest of the Palestinian coastland. In August 1189 he marched on Acre and laid the important port-city under a blockade. Saladin brought up his forces later in the same month. On 4 October a battle took place, which was essentially indecisive as the two sides settled back into their old positions.

The news of the sudden and generally unexpected collapse of the kingdom and of Saladin's capture of the Holy City itself stimulated a response in Western Europe that produced the Third Crusade. The call to the Crusade was sent out by Pope Clement III, and it was first answered by the senior Western ruler, the Holy Roman Emperor Frederick I Barbarossa. But he was never to reach Palestine. On his long journey overland to the East he was drowned in the Göksu river on 10 June 1190 as he approached Silifke. Although the German army went on to the Holy Land, it dwindled as it advanced and formed only a contingent of the Crusading forces. The great body of these were English and French, and were led by the two kings, Richard Lionheart and Philip II Augustus respectively. They made their way by sea and landed directly at the centre of the contest, the camp outside Acre, Philip on 20 April 1191 and Richard on 8 June. On 12 July the Muslim garrison of Acre offered to capitulate as Saladin had failed to help them in their extremity. The capitulation was accepted, and on 12 July the kings of England and France entered the city. Early in August, however, Philip set sail for France, and for the next 14 months the history of the Third Crusade is the history of the confrontation of Richard and Saladin.

On 22 August 1191 Richard left Acre, after first massacring his Muslim prisoners, even while he was actually negotiating with Saladin about their release. His primary aim was to reconquer Jerusalem, but first he had to secure his position in the coastlands. As he moved southwards he was confronted by the Muslim forces under Saladin near to Arsūf, where a pitched battle took place on 7 September. Richard was victorious and continued his march to Jaffa, where he reconstructed the fortifications. Negotiations with Saladin were resumed, and on 20 October Richard suggested that Saladin's brother, al-ʿĀdil Sayf al-Dīn (known to the Franks as Saphadin) should marry Richard's sister Joanna, formerly queen of Sicily, and that the two should rule over a reunited Palestine from Jerusalem. The plan, if it was seriously intended, was wrecked by Joanna's refusal to marry a Muslim, and al-ʿĀdil rejected an alternative suggestion that he should become a Christian. Conrad of Montferrat, in the meanwhile, was negotiating separately with Saladin.

When in November 1191 Saladin withdrew to winter quarters in Jerusalem, Richard occupied al-Ramla and then moved up to al-Latrūn for Christmas. Then, in spite of stormy weather, he advanced to Bayt

Nūba, about 19 km from Jerusalem, on 3 January 1192. Here he was dissuaded from going on, and he withdrew to the coastland. There he advanced to Ascalon, and restored this important fortress. But his position was weakening. Money for paying the troops was running out, while Conrad, secure in his hold over Tyre, refused to cooperate with Richard and his protégé, King Guy.

The time was approaching for Richard to disengage himself from the Holy Land and its problems. First the future of the kingdom had to be decided. In April 1192 a council of the Frankish nobility was invited to choose between Guy of Lusignan and Conrad of Montferrat as king. To Richard's embarrassment they chose Conrad, who had already in 1190 married Isabel, the sister of Sibyl and heiress of the kingdom. But Conrad's reign was to be short. On 28 April he was killed by an Isma'ili assassin, and the kingship was again vacant. The problem was solved when, by a hasty remarriage on 5 May 1192, Isabel brought the illusory crown of Jerusalem to a new husband, Henry of Champagne. He had come to Acre as a Crusader in 1190. As the nephew of both Richard and Philip, he had from the start occupied a high position among the Frankish nobles. As a consolation prize, Guy of Lusignan was given Cyprus, which Richard had conquered from its Byzantine ruler on his way to Acre.

To extricate himself from Palestine, Richard needed a settlement with Saladin. He was in close touch with al-'Ādil and in March 1192 agreement seemed to be near. However the report of a revolt by one of Saladin's nephews led Richard to attack and capture Dārūm, the most southerly fortress on the Palestinian coast, in May. Then once more Richard marched on Jerusalem. On 11 June he again reached Bayt Nūba and caught a distant glimpse of the Holy City. But although Saladin prepared for the defence of Jerusalem, Richard was forced to realise that he had not the means to capture and hold the city, and early in July he withdrew to the coast. There were further hostilities, but on 2 September 1192 a truce was finally concluded. The coastal cities as far as Jaffa were to be under Frankish rule, Christian pilgrims were to have free access to the holy places, and both Muslims and Christians were to have freedom of passage through each other's territory. The great fortress of Ascalon was to be demolished.

On these terms the restored Latin kingdom, still nominally of Jerusalem, was established. Richard sailed from Acre on 9 October 1192, and met his death fighting in France in 1199. Saladin died in the odour of sanctity on 4 March 1193, leaving the unstable family confederacy of the Ayyubids to dominate the Near East and to continue to confront the Franks.

Notes

1. Gibb, *Damascus Chronicle*, p. 299.
2. Gibb, *Damascus Chronicle*, p. 304.
3. Gibb, *Damascus Chronicle*, p. 310.
4. Ibn al-Athīr, *al-Bāhir*, ed. Ṭulaymāt, tr. P. M. Holt, Cairo and Baghdad, 1963, p. 106.

chapter five

THE FRANKISH STATES AND THE LATER AYYUBIDS

The Ayyubid realm and the Latin kingdom

With the ending of the Third Crusade by Richard's truce with Saladin, and with Saladin's death in 1193, a new and much more relaxed relationship developed between the Frankish states and their Muslim neighbours. The Ayyubids were in some respects an intrusive Kurdish clan, who under Saladin had taken over the Turkish Zangid realm and Arab Egypt. They were largely self-contained, intermarrying, and after Saladin's death little concerned with hostilities against the Latin kingdom, now diminished to a strip of the Palestinian coastland with its capital at Acre.

During his lifetime Saladin had appointed his sons to govern as his deputies in the principal territories of his realm, and they continued briefly as quasi-independent rulers after his death. Soon however a paramount chief of the Ayyubid clan emerged in the person of Saladin's brother and chief assistant, al-ʿĀdil Sayf al-Dīn, who had governed the fringe territory of al-Jazīra, i.e. northern Mesopotamia. In 1196 he occupied Damascus, and from 1195 onwards he controlled Egypt, from 1200 as its sultan. He went on to make a new territorial settlement for the benefit of his own sons. The direct descendants of Saladin were displaced, only al-Ẓāhir Ghāzī and his progeny being left in Aleppo to control northern Syria. Al-ʿĀdil was succeeded as sultan of Egypt and paramount chief of the Ayyubids by his son al-Kāmil Muḥammad, who ruled until 1238. After an episode of dynastic troubles, Egypt and the paramountcy passed to a son of al-Kāmil, al-Ṣāliḥ Ayyūb, who ruled from 1240 to 1249. He was the creator of a Mamluk corps which after his death was to dominate Egypt.

The Latin kingdom in the meantime, originally restricted to a trucial coastland from Jaffa to Tyre, succeeded in 1197 in acquiring Sidon, Beirut and Jubayl (the Gibelet of the Franks), thus closing the gap with the county of Tripoli to the north. This was accomplished with the help of German Crusaders sent by the Emperor Henry VI, who had hoped to continue the project of his father, Frederick Barbarossa, but died in 1197 at Messina. On the whole the Frankish states were content in these years to coexist with their Ayyubid neighbours, while al-ʿĀdil for his part was anxious to avoid the heavy cost of warfare as Saladin had experienced it. He wished to avoid provoking another Crusade, but Crusaders arrived, repugnant to al-ʿĀdil and not wholly welcome to the Frankish states. It is to these interventions from Western Europe that we must turn in order to consider the military and diplomatic relationships of the period.

The Fifth Crusade: 1217–21

The Fifth Crusade was vigorously initiated by Pope Innocent III (d. 1216) and subsequently supported by his successor, Honorius III (1216–27). The papal legate, Cardinal Pelagius of Albano, who was chosen by Honorius to direct the operations of the Crusade, played a very prominent part in events. In contrast to previous Crusades the expedition was chiefly supported by commoners, as the knightly class was poorly represented.

The early operations of the Crusaders in Palestine, where aid was given by troops recruited by King Andrew of Hungary, were largely ineffective, and in 1218 the Crusaders decided to strike at Egypt, the centre of Ayyubid power. In so doing they picked up a plan originally formulated by John of Brienne, the king of Jerusalem, in concert with the military orders. This then was in substance the first Egyptian Crusade.

In May 1218 the Crusaders arrived by sea at the harbour of Damietta, at the end of the eastern branch of the Nile. There they elected King John to command the enterprise. From a military standpoint Damietta was a well-defended city, protected by a triple wall, while on an island in midstream an isolated tower, the Tower of the Chain, was the base for huge iron chains to bar passage up and down the river. The Crusaders concentrated their efforts on the capture of this strong point. They took the Tower of the Chain on 25 August 1218. The news reached al-ʿĀdil on his deathbed, and henceforth the response to the Crusaders was in the hands of his son, al-Kāmil.

After the capture of the Tower of the Chain, the Crusaders were inactive and awaited reinforcements. Cardinal Pelagius arrived in September, to rival King John in the command. Al-Kāmil in the meantime had established himself in the vicinity of Damietta, which he was preparing to defend. In February 1219 he opened negotiations with the Crusaders as he was desperate to get them out of Egypt. He offered them the retrocession of the whole territory of the kingdom of Jerusalem with the exception of the two Transjordanian fortresses of al-Karak and al-Shawbak, and also a truce for 30 years. King John would have accepted the offer but he was overruled by Pelagius. Again at the end of August, when Damietta was suffering severely from the Crusaders' attacks, al-Kāmil renewed the offer, and once more Pelagius overruled King John. A third attempt at negotiation at the beginning of October again broke on the rock of Pelagius's opposition. On 5 November 1219 Damietta fell and was sacked by the Crusaders, and al-Kāmil withdrew to al-Manṣūra, about 60 km upstream. A year of inactivity followed, while King John left to pursue a claim to the crown of Armenia.

After the loss of Damietta al-Kāmil, who was building up an encampment and town at al-Manṣūra, again offered to retrocede to the Franks all the territory that Saladin had conquered from them except the Transjordanian strongholds. Pelagius again rejected the offer, as he now thought that the Crusaders would be able to conquer the whole of Egypt and Jerusalem as well. He was expecting the arrival of fresh reinforcements under the Emperor Frederick II of Hohenstaufen. The troops arrived in May 1221, but not the emperor, and in the following month the Crusaders began to move. They had been rejoined by King John, as ever a dissident from Pelagius over strategy. A combined military and naval force moved upstream to the vicinity of al-Manṣūra. Muslim ships thereupon blocked it off from its base at Damietta, while the Crusaders in attempting a retreat by land on 26 August were thwarted by the flooding of the Nile. They were forced to negotiate with al-Kāmil, offering the return of Damietta in exchange for freedom of withdrawal from Egypt. A settlement that allowed the withdrawal and established a truce for eight years was finally agreed on 30 August 1221. So the Fifth Crusade came to its ignominious end.

The Crusade of Frederick II: 1228–9

The Emperor Frederick II first undertook the obligation to go on Crusade when he was crowned king of Germany at Aachen on 15 July 1215. His act surprised Pope Innocent III, who was then initiating preparations for the Fifth Crusade, and 13 years were to elapse before Frederick finally carried out his obligations. The reasons for this delay centred primarily in Germany, where Frederick's position was not at first secure, and his situation was complicated by his possession of Sicily, which he had inherited through his mother, Constance. His youthful vow (he was 20 years old at the time) was at first disregarded, but in 1218, when the Crusaders under Pelagius expected reinforcements, he was pressed to take action by Pope Honorius III, who had on previous occasions agreed to repeated postponements. As has been mentioned, Frederick sent an army of Crusaders to Damietta in 1221, but did not go in person.

Two developments brought the situation in the Near East to the forefront. In 1225 there were negotiations for Frederick's marriage to Isabel (also known as Yolanda), the daughter of King John of Jerusalem. Frederick's first wife had died in 1222, and this second marriage was carried out by proxy in Acre, whence Isabel sailed in August 1225. As the ultimate heir to the titular crown of Jerusalem, Frederick now had a stimulus to undertake a Crusade.

The more important development was the estrangement of the Sultan al-Kāmil from his brother al-Muʿaẓẓam ʿĪsā, the ruler of Damascus. In an unprecedented move, al-Kāmil sent an envoy to invite Frederick to come as his ally to Acre, promising to grant him Jerusalem and other cities in recompense. His envoy was the amir Fakhr al-Dīn Ibn al-Shaykh, who in due course received the honour of knighthood from the Christian ruler while remaining a Muslim. Al-Kāmil's offer to Frederick was always somewhat shadowy, since Jerusalem was not his to give, being in the possession of al-Muʿaẓẓam. Frederick nevertheless set out in June 1228 in defiance of a ban by Pope Gregory IX, so that even technically his expedition could not be called a Crusade. It was in any case rather of the nature of a state visit to a fellow sovereign. He left Europe knowing himself to be at a disadvantage, since al-Muʿaẓẓam had died in November 1227, leaving as his heir a young prince who was likely to be amenable to al-Kāmil's guidance.

Frederick reached Acre on 7 September 1228, to find himself not wholly welcome to the Franks and something of an embarrassment to al-Kāmil. He was personally agreeable to the Muslims, who appreciated him because he was well educated, intelligent and a sceptic in matters of religion. Al-Kāmil avoided meeting him, and was evasive about the promised cession of Jerusalem and other Palestinian territory. Further negotiations took place, and by the settlement of 18 February 1229 Frederick received Jerusalem with permission to restore its fortifications, and also Bethlehem, Nazareth and a corridor linking Jerusalem to the Frankish coast. There was however one important reservation. The Muslim Holy Places containing the Dome of the Rock and al-Aqṣā mosque were excluded from the grant. There was also to be a truce for ten years. The cession of Jerusalem was offensive to Muslims; the reservation of the Holy Places equally so to Christians.

Frederick made his state entry into Jerusalem on 17 March 1229 and on the next day, a Sunday, he wore his crown in the Church of the Holy Sepulchre. No mass was celebrated and no clergy were present, in accordance with the papal ban. Having thus achieved the perpetual hope of all Crusaders – the restitution of Jerusalem to Christian rule – Frederick set about making preparations for an immediate departure. This was probably to secure his position in Sicily; the Holy Land was always a sideshow to more pressing European interests. He embarked at Acre on 1 May 1229 after a humiliating display of the popular dislike, and landed at Brindisi on 10 June. Frederick's 'Crusade' was over. His great achievement, the regaining of Jerusalem, was of but short duration. When the truce made with al-Kāmil expired in 1239, al-Nāṣir Dā'ūd, the son of al-Muʿaẓẓam 'Īsā and ruler of eastern Palestine and Transjordan, reoccupied the city on 7 December 1239.

The Crusade of Theobald of Champagne and Richard of Cornwall: 1239–41

The two leaders of this Crusade, who never met during its course, were Theobald, king of Navarre and count of Champagne, and Richard Plantagenet, earl of Cornwall and brother of King Henry III of England. Isabella, Richard and Henry's sister, became the Emperor Frederick II's third wife in 1235. Theobald and Richard both took the cross in response to Pope Gregory IX's call in 1234 for Crusaders from England and France to aid Jerusalem when the truce made by al-Kāmil and Frederick expired in 1239. Later the pope expressed the hope of having an army of Crusaders in the Holy Land for ten years after the end of the truce.

After various postponements, the date for starting was set for August 1239. What ensued was a Crusade in two acts. First came the French act, when Theobald and his Crusaders assembled in September 1239 at Acre, where they were joined by the local Frankish magnates. Meanwhile the Muslims attacked Jerusalem, still a Christian city, which had not however been effectively refortified during or after Frederick II's visit. While it was Theobald's wish to deal with this urgent threat, it was decided in a joint council with the Frankish leaders to advance down the coast to Ascalon and build a castle there, whence they hoped in defiance of topography to march on Damascus. The movement southwards began on 2 November, and ten days later the Crusaders reached Jaffa. There they learned that al-Kāmil had sent a force to Gaza to guard his Egyptian frontier. A group of French and local barons decided to go forward and engage with the Muslim army before rejoining their comrades at Ascalon. They were surprised and attacked by the Muslims, who then retired, while the Crusaders returned to Ascalon. The whole force fell back to Jaffa and then to Acre, leaving the castle unbuilt.

When al-Nāṣir Dā'ūd reoccupied Jerusalem as mentioned above, the Crusaders, who had spent a month relaxing in Acre, were stirred into fresh activity. Hostility among the Ayyubids led one of their princes, al-Muẓaffar Taqī al-Dīn, the ruler of Ḥamāh, to seek Theobald's help. He offered to surrender and accept conversion. Theobald advanced into the county of Tripoli, but al-Muẓaffar's offer was suddenly withdrawn as Theobald's movement in itself relieved him from his opponents' pressure.

Soon another offer came. This time it was from al-Ṣāliḥ Ismā'īl, the ruler of Damascus, who had driven out his predecessor there, his nephew al-Ṣāliḥ Ayyūb. In the kaleidoscope of Ayyubid politics al-Ṣāliḥ Ayyūb had now become ruler of Egypt. Al-Ṣāliḥ Ismā'īl, feeling himself threatened, offered to return Galilee, Jerusalem and territory around Gaza if the Crusaders would help him against al-Ṣāliḥ Ayyūb. Theobald agreed, and the Crusaders set forth to cooperate with one Muslim faction against another. Their force combined with that of al-Ṣāliḥ Ismā'īl near Jaffa, on which an army from Egypt advanced. Large-scale desertions from the Damascene to the Egyptian side left the Crusaders without an ally, and they took refuge in Ascalon. Theobald now made a truce with al-Ṣāliḥ Ayyūb, which confirmed the cessions of territory promised by al-Ṣāliḥ Ismā'īl, although it was opposed by some of the local Frankish lords. This enabled Theobald, who was weary of the enterprise, to make a pilgrimage to Jerusalem and then sail from Acre in September 1240. Although all the French Crusaders did not leave with him, this was the end of his Crusade.

The English Crusade under Richard of Cornwall was to all intents and purposes a separate enterprise. Richard sailed from Marseilles in September 1240 and reached Acre on 8 October. He marched to Jaffa, where he found the envoys of al-Ṣāliḥ Ayyūb ready to confirm the truce earlier made with Theobald. This really left them with very little to do except to await al-Ṣāliḥ Ayyūb's final ratification, which was reported to Richard on 8 February 1241, and to complete the rebuilding of Richard the Lionheart's castle at Ascalon. This was done by mid-March, and on 13 April an exchange of Christian and Muslim prisoners took place under the truce. On 3 May Richard of Cornwall sailed from Acre, and this Crusade in two acts came to an end.

The Crusade of St Louis of France: 1248–50

The last Crusade in the Ayyubid period was led by St Louis, King Louis IX of France, between 1248 and 1250. In the course of events this expedition followed very much the pattern of the Fifth Crusade. The Crusaders were Frenchmen under noble leaders, and an important source of information about the Crusade is the biography of St Louis by Jean de Joinville, who accompanied him on the expedition. This work is explicitly a panegyric of the king. Arabic sources counterbalance and correct Joinville's account.

The Crusade sailed from Marseilles and passed the winter of 1248–9 in Cyprus. While there, Louis received an envoy from 'the great King of the Tartars', i.e. the Great Khan of the Mongols. The Great Khan Güyük, who was sympathetic to Christianity, had died in April 1248, and there was at this time an interregnum until Möngke was elected as Great Khan in 1251. The envoy may in fact have been sent to engage the attention of an important Christian monarch. Louis sent in return a tent of fine scarlet cloth arranged as a chapel with religious images carved in stone. His envoys were two Franciscan friars who knew the Mongol language.

The king and his Crusaders sailed from Cyprus in May 1249 and made their landfall at Damietta on 5 June. Al-Ṣāliḥ Ayyūb, who held the Ayyubid paramountcy, was a dying man, but he hastened to Egypt to head the Muslim resistance, which as before centred in the camp-city of al-Manṣūra. Damietta itself had been evacuated before the arrival of the Crusaders, who occupied it without difficulty. It became their base and the queen of France's residence. When the Nile flood subsided in October, Louis began his advance southwards along the Nile. Reinforcements arrived from France, and after some fighting the Crusaders encamped outside al-Manṣūra. This remained the situation until February 1250, when an Egyptian showed the Crusaders a ford by which the bulk of the army, headed by the king and his brother, Robert of Artois, crossed the river. In the ensuing battle Robert of Artois, disobeying the king's instructions, led an impetuous charge into al-Manṣūra and was killed in its narrow streets. Louis won the battle and encamped outside al-Manṣūra, where he remained for eight weeks. In April 1250 he decided to withdraw to Damietta and open negotiations with the enemy command. But on the Muslim side significant changes were in progress. On 6 April Louis was captured, and shortly afterwards his troops laid down their arms in response to an order feigned to come from the king.

Sultan al-Ṣāliḥ Ayyūb had died in his camp by al-Manṣūra in November 1249. His son and heir, al-Muʿaẓẓam Tūrān–Shāh, had to be summoned from his distant apanage of Ḥiṣn Kayfā, the modern Hasankeyf in Turkey. During this crucial interregnum the military situation was saved by the resolute action of his wife, his former concubine, a Turkish woman named Shajar al-Durr, in cooperation with the commanding officer of the troops, the amir and Muslim knight, Fakhr al-Dīn Ibn al-Shaykh. The sultan's death was concealed, and orders to which Shajar al-Durr forged his signature continued to be issued. An oath of loyalty to al-Ṣāliḥ Ayyūb and al-Mu'aẓẓam Tūrān-Shāh was imposed. Shajar al-Durr, herself by origin a *mamlūka*, stood in a particularly close relationship to the Baḥriyya, the Kipchak Turkish Mamluks who formed al-Ṣāliḥ Ayyūb's elite corps. The political as well as the military importance of the Baḥriyya presumably increased when Fakhr al-Dīn, who was not a Mamluk, was killed in the fighting at al-Manṣūra on 9 February 1250.

Tūrān-Shāh arrived at al-Manṣūra on 25 February, and intended to march on Damietta. He encamped on the way at Faraskūr, and there he met his end. He lacked his father's energy, and from the time of his arrival in Egypt he never ceased to give offence to the Mamluks. This opened up a succession crisis such as was to be a recurrent feature of Egyptian history over the next two and a half centuries. Tūrān-Shāh sought to install his own followers in place of the chief Mamluk officers of al-Ṣāliḥ's household, appointing an Abyssinian slave as his head of security and a eunuch as his steward. In a drunken fit he struck the tops off the candles with his sword, threatening so to behead the Baḥriyya. He disparaged and threatened Shajar al-Durr, who had preserved the realm for him. Debauchery rather than warfare was his way of life, and a Mamluk conspiracy ensued. He was attacked and killed after a feast on or about 1 May 1250.

A transitional period of nearly three months followed, when Shajar al-Durr reigned, uniquely in Egyptian Muslim history, as 'Queen of the Muslims' (*Malikat al-Muslimīn*). After this a Mamluk amir, Aybak al-Turkumānī, was installed as sultan of Egypt with the royal title of al-Malik al-Mu'izz. So the Arab Fatimid caliphate and the Kurdish Ayyubid sultanate gave place to the rule of the Turks, which was to last, at least ostensibly, until the end of the dynasty founded by Muḥammad 'Alī Pasha and the declaration of the Egyptian Republic by Gamāl 'Abd al-Nāṣir in 1953.

The aftermath

The death of al-Ṣāliḥ Ayyūb and the subsequent coup by the Baḥriyya marked the beginning of the end of Ayyubid rule. After the loss of Egypt to the Mamluks, the Ayyubids continued to hold for a time their Syrian principalities. The end there came in 1260 with a Mongol invasion of Syria, followed by the defeat of the Mongols by a Mamluk expeditionary force at 'Ayn Jālūt in Palestine on 3 September of the same year. Thereafter Muslim Syria was annexed by the Mamluk sultanate, under which only the small and inoffensive principality of Ḥamāh survived under Ayyubid rule for some 80 years. Its penultimate prince was the chronicler and geographer Ismāʿīl Abu'l-Fidā'.

To the Franks, the emergence of the Mamluk sultanate of Egypt and Syria meant the appearance of a new and aggressive opponent. The tolerable coexistence of the Frankish states and the Ayyubid principalities, punctuated only by intrusive crusades from Europe, was at an end, superseded by the hostility of first-generation Turkish converts to Islam bent on reviving the *jihād*.

chapter six

THE FRANKISH STATES AND THE EARLY MAMLUK SULTANS

The extension of Mamluk rule to Syria

Since the Mamluk seizure of political power in Egypt in 1250, after al-Ṣāliḥ Ayyūb's dying leadership of the Muslim resistance to the Crusade of Louis IX, it might have been expected that the Mamluks as young and fanatical converts to Islam would have come out at once on *jihād* against the Franks. That this did not take place for 13 years was primarily due to two factors.

The first of these was that although the Mamluks held Egypt, Muslim Syria was still controlled by the Ayyubid princes. Chief among them was Saladin's great-grandson, al-Nāṣir Yūsuf, who held Aleppo in succession to his father from 1236, and in 1250 acquired Damascus, which thenceforward was his capital. In 1251 he invaded Egypt to overthrow the Mamluk sultanate, but was defeated by Aybak at al-ʿAbbāsa on the eastern approaches to the Delta. In 1256 the Caliph al-Mustaʿṣim negotiated a fragile peace treaty between Aybak and al-Nāṣir Yūsuf. Meanwhile factional quarrels among the Baḥriyya had led to the flight of some of their number to Ayyubid Syria, where they endeavoured to instigate first al-Nāṣir Yūsuf, then al-Mughīth ʿUmar, the lord of al-Karak, against their opponents in Egypt. Dissension and jealousy between Aybak and Shajar al-Durr, whom he had married in 1250, resulted in the violent deaths of both of them in 1257, and the government of Egypt was taken by Quṭuz, one of Aybak's Mamluks, at first in the name of Aybak's young son.

The polarisation of Mamluk Egypt and Ayyubid Syria was suddenly ended by the violent irruption of a third force, the world-conquering Mongols from the East. Möngke, mentioned in the previous chapter, was elected Great Khan in 1251, and in 1255 he sent his brother, Hülegü, to conquer the lands of the Near East. In 1258 Baghdad was captured, and its last caliph, al-Mustaʿṣim, met his end. Al-Nāṣir Yūsuf deemed it advisable to send gifts to Hülegü, but his envoy returned with a menacing and humiliating letter. Hülegü proceeded to march on Aleppo, which fell in January 1260. Al-Nāṣir Yūsuf fled but was captured and sent to Hülegü, and in March Damascus fell. At this point Hülegü learnt of Möngke's death, and left Syria to participate in the settlement of the succession. He left his army in the charge of his general, Kitbugha Noyon.

These events had their repercussions on the Frankish states. Not only did the Franks see the gratifying spectacle of the downfall of Muslim power before the Mongols, they also knew that the Mongols were tolerant towards and sometimes favourable to Christianity. A number of the mothers and wives of Hülegü and his successors, the *īl-khāns* of Persia, were Christians, as was also Möngke's mother. During the episode of Mongol domination in Syria, Bohemond VI of Antioch and Tripoli was their ally, although the Latin kingdom had remained aloof.

The power of the Mongols in Syria ended as suddenly as it had begun. The leader of the Baḥriyya exiles in Syria, a young Mamluk named Baybars al-Bunduqdārī, reached agreement with his rival in Egypt, Quṭuz, who had usurped the sultanate in the face of the Mongol threat. As the Egyptian army entered Palestine, Baybars led an advance force that confronted and routed Kitbugha Noyon at the battle of ʿAyn Jālūt fought in the vale of Jezreel, north of Mount Gilboa, on 3 September 1260. So ended the immediate Mongol threat to Syria and Egypt, although it long remained in the background. When the combined forces of Quṭuz and Baybars were returning to Egypt, there was a factional conspiracy in which Quṭuz was killed on 24 October. The fatal blow was probably struck by Baybars himself. At any rate he did not hesitate to claim the sultanate, and his claim was accepted by the other Mamluk grandees.

The sultanate of Baybars

In this way Sultan Baybars came to the throne. He assumed the royal title of al-Malik al-Ẓāhir, 'the Manifest King'. It was a curious, if unconscious, echo of the title borne by a distant Hellenistic predecessor in Syria, Antiochus IV Epiphanes. It was three years before Baybars could begin his *jihād* against the Frankish states. He did not gain control over Syria until 1263, having, amongst other difficulties, to defeat a Mamluk rival, Sanjar al-Ḥalabī, who had been appointed governor of Damascus by Quṭuz and now declared himself sultan. Also al-Mughīth ʿUmar of al-Karak, once Baybars's ally, now threatened his hold over Syria, and was not captured and removed frown power until April 1263.

Thereafter successive hammer blows fell on Baybars's Frankish enemies. In 1263 he destroyed the church at Nazareth, described by his contemporary biographer Ibn 'Abd al-Ẓāhir as 'the greatest of their places of worship where they claim the Christian religion to have originated'. He sent a raiding force into the vicinity of Acre, and followed this up by leading an expedition from his base-camp by Mount Tabor, which enabled him to make a thorough reconnaissance of the Frankish capital. In 1265 he made a second expedition against the Franks. Advancing by the Palestinian coastland, he fell upon Caesarea in February and besieged the city. The citadel resisted, but finally surrendered on 5 March 1265. The place was demolished, so that it could not serve as a base for Crusaders arriving from overseas. A detachment of the Mamluk army then captured and devastated Haifa. Baybars meanwhile advanced to Arsūf on 21 March, and laid the city under siege. It fell on 26 April, and as it was a coastal city like Caesarea, it was also demolished. To secure the extensive coastal territories that had now come into his hands, Baybars distributed the land with certificates of ownership to his amirs and followers.

In 1266 Baybars made his objective an important inland stronghold, the Templars' castle at Ṣafad in the hills of Galilee. An advance party was sent to keep it under surveillance while the sultan brought up his siege-train from a base-camp near Acre. He arrived on 13 June, and the siege began a fortnight later. The garrison surrendered on 23 July, and were put to death on the following day, the pretext being that they had broken the terms of an informal safe conduct. Unlike the coastal cities, Ṣafad was not demolished. The stronghold was refurbished and provided with a Muslim garrison. Two other strongholds, Ḥūnīn and Tibnīn (Le Toron of the Franks) both lying inland from Tyre, were surrendered to Baybars in the same year.

In February 1268 Baybars set out again for Syria and made his way to Ṣafad to supervise its restoration. While he was there an envoy arrived from Guy of Ibelin, the count of Jaffa, asking for a renewal of the truce Baybars had made with his father. Baybars refused this, but offered a safe conduct in return for the surrender of the city. Jaffa was handed over on 8 March, and like the other coastal cities it was demolished. In contrast, Shaqīf Arnūn, the Templar castle of Belfort, dominating the point at which the Līṭānī river turns sharply to the west, was restored after its capture on 15 April. Baybars went on to his greatest triumph when he besieged and took Antioch. The city was attacked on 18 May and the garrison in the citadel surrendered on the following day. Much booty was taken, and both city and citadel were devastated by fire.

During 1270 word reached Baybars that Louis IX of France had resolved upon another Crusade to avenge his defeat at Damietta. The king was advised first to take Tunis, then to advance by sea and land to Egypt. Owing to the king's death in an epidemic of plague during the siege of Tunis, this ambitious plan came to nothing, and Baybars was left in safety.

Baybars's last successes against the Frankish states were achieved in 1271, when he led his army against the Hospitaller castle of Crac des Chevaliers (to the Muslims Ḥiṣn al-Akrād) in the Syrian hill-country between Ḥimṣ and the sea. The siege began on 14 March and ended with the surrender of the garrison and their departure under safe conduct on 7 April. With its fall, Tripoli was endangered, but Baybars was constrained to grant a truce to Count Bohemond VI as he heard that an English Crusading army had arrived. Its commander was the Lord Edward, the son and later the successor of King Henry III. Edward hoped to use his forces in a joint operation with the Mongols of Abaqa, the son of Hülegü and his successor as *īl-khān* of Persia. The scheme proved illusory, and Edward left Acre in September 1272, becoming king of England while on the way home.

The sultanate of Qalāwūn

Although Baybars, hoping to establish a hereditary sultanate, had arranged years previously for the succession of his eldest son, this project quickly failed. On Baybars's death in July 1277 the most powerful grandee in the realm was his former comrade in arms, Qalāwūn al-Alfī, i.e. 'the Thousander', whose nickname indicated the high price of 1,000 dinars paid for him by his first master. In 1279 Qalāwūn set Baybars's sons aside and usurped the throne. Like Baybars before him however he was confronted by a rival in Damascus, the governor Sunqur al-Ashqar, while Baybars's sons maintained a royal court in exile in the stronghold of al-Karak. These difficulties were gradually overcome. Sunqur was defeated and driven out of Damascus in 1280. A Mongol invasion of Syria sent by the *Īl-khān* Abaqa was defeated in 1281 at Ḥimṣ. Finally early in 1286 al-Karak capitulated and the two remaining sons of Baybars were brought to Cairo.

By this time Qalāwūn was able to turn to the *jihād* against the Franks. He began in April 1285, when he captured the Hospitallers' castle of Margat (Arabic, al-Marqab) lying inland south of Latakia. He re-established it with a Mamluk garrison but demolished another Hospitaller stronghold at Maraclea (Arabic, Maraqiyya), which lay on the coast. The two Frankish states still remaining were the county of Tripoli and the Latin Kingdom. Both were in a curious political situation. Since the death of the last hereditary count of Tripoli, Bohemond VII, with whom Qalāwūn had made a treaty in 1281, the territory had been held by the lord of Gibelet (Arabic, Jubayl), Bartolomeo Embriaco, who was of Genoese origin, and so was distrusted by the Venetians. His position was challenged by the sister of Bohemond VII, and envoys from Tripoli invited Qalāwūn to intervene. He did not hesitate to act, and in April 1289 took the city of Tripoli and demolished it, so ending the Frankish hold over that part of the coast.

There remained the Latin kingdom. At a rather earlier date the crown of Jerusalem had been in dispute but in 1286 Henry of Lusignan, the king of Cyprus, had been recognised as king of Jerusalem and crowned in the cathedral of Tyre. In 1283 Qalāwūn had made a treaty with 'the authorities in the kingdom of Acre', who were specified as the *bailli* or regent of the kingdom, and the masters of the three military orders, i.e. the Templars, Hospitallers and Teutonic Knights. The treaty was to last for ten years, months, days and hours from 3 June 1283, and the territory held by the kingdom was specified in detail. Two solemn and lengthy oaths of ratification were appended to the treaty.

This ten-year truce was obviously an obstacle to Qalāwūn when he wished to follow up his victory over Tripoli with a final campaign against Acre. The sultan found a *casus belli* in the killing of some Muslims in Acre by Christians. Various accounts are given of this incident, but when Qalāwūn called a council of his amirs he came up against their unexpected scruples. He thereupon instructed his secretary of state, Fatḥ al-Dīn Ibn 'Abd al-Ẓāhir, to see if there was any escape clause in the treaty. Fatḥ al-Dīn discussed the matter with his experienced father, but failed to find a way out. However, his cousin, Shāfiʿ b. 'Alī al-'Asqalānī (who depicts himself as ever fertile in expedients) rose to the occasion by declaring, 'We are with the sultan. If he prefers abrogation [of the treaty], it is abrogated; and if he prefers continuation, it shall continue.' On being told that 'the amirs have grown old and lazy, and the sultan would prefer abrogation', he selected a relevant clause, although he differs as to which one in the two accounts he gives of this affair.[1] In any case, Qalāwūn set out forthwith, only to die suddenly on 12 November 1290 as the army left Cairo. The expedition was nevertheless brought to a victorious conclusion by his son and successor, al-Ashraf Khalīl. Acre fell to him on 18 May 1291, and mopping-up operations soon cleared the Franks out of their remaining footholds on the coast. So ended the Latin kingdom of Jerusalem, almost 200 years after Urban II at Clermont had called the First Crusade into existence.

Note

1. P. M. Holt, 'Mamluk-Frankish diplomatic relations in the reign of Qalāwūn, *Journal of the Royal Asiatic Society*, 2, 1989, p. 289.

CONCLUSION

The conquest of Acre and the last Frankish territories in 1291 by al-Ashraf Khalīl meant not only the disappearance of the Latin kingdom from the map, but also the loss and demolition of the ports of Syria-Palestine that might serve as bases for Crusaders bent on its restoration. People in Western Europe were loath to give up the hope that all might be regained. One indication of this was the abundant production of 'recovery treatises', some of which gave careful consideration to the strategy and tactics of renewed Crusading ventures. Successive popes showed their commitment to the launching of a Crusade; only an appropriate leader was lacking.

Around 1305 it seemed that aspirations might result in action. A new pope, Clement V, was elected in that year, while the king of France, Philip IV the Fair, who lost his wife in 1305 also, became notably pious. This piety led him on the one hand to claim the lay leadership of the Crusading movement, on the other to suppress the wealthy order of the Templars. He took the cross at a splendid festival in 1313, but there was no practical outcome to this magnificent display of zeal. Both he and Pope Clement died in 1314, summoned before the throne of God, according to legend, by their victim, Jacques de Molay, the last Master of the Temple.

Although planning for a Crusade continued under Philip's three successors, the practical difficulties and the expense of such a venture ultimately defeated all its advocates. A more active cause of concern also intervened with the outbreak of the long period of hostilities between England and France, the so-called Hundred Years War, in 1337. In 1365 the last Crusade in the Near East took place when Peter I of Lusignan, king of Cyprus, who had a hereditary claim to the crown of Jerusalem, led an expedition against Alexandria, which might be called the third and last Egyptian Crusade. Alexandria was captured, but the success could be neither exploited nor maintained. A week later the victorious Crusaders evacuated the city and returned to Cyprus. Henceforward the growing power of the Ottoman Turks was to be the main preoccupation of Christian European states.

The claim of the Lusignan kings of Cyprus to be the rightful kings of Jerusalem had a ghostly after-life in an Arabic historical legend, which is recounted by several writers but apparently lacks any Western corroboration. A rambling Arabic account of King Peter I's expedition to Alexandria gives this version of the legend:

> When Peter, the lord of Cyprus (may God curse him), succeeded to the throne on the perdition of his father, Hugh [King Hugh IV], he sent to ask the Sultan al-Malik al-Nāṣir Ḥasan to give him permission to go to the town of Tyre on the Syrian coast, so that he might be seated on a column there as is customary with all who become kings of the island of Cyprus. For the kingship of it would only be complete, as they claim, by his being seated on that column or a place reserved for the seating of the king, so that thereby his kingship might be complete and the execution of his judgment among his subjects might be valid. The sultan viewed him with contempt, and forbade him to enter the town of Tyre; so that (and God knows best) was a reason for his raid on Alexandria.[1]

From the time of the First Crusade, the warfare in the Near East to gain, hold or recover Jerusalem had possessed a specific quality to Christian eyes. This outlook was lacking to contemporary Muslims. Admittedly Christian aggression and conquest provoked Holy War, *jihād*, and certainly Jerusalem was regarded as the third Holy City of Islam, but although the hostilities in Syria-Palestine are described in Muslim historical works, they are not as such the special subject of any contemporary chronicle. The first specific Muslim account of the Crusades is entitled *al-I'lām wa'l-tabyīn fī khurūj al-Firanj al-malā'īn 'alā diyār al-Muslimīn*, 'Information and exposition concerning the aggression of the accursed Franks on the homelands of the Muslims', by Aḥmad b. 'Alī al-Ḥarīrī. Its date is significant. It was completed in late Shawwāl 926, i.e. between 3 and 12 October 1520. Another short Arabic work of this period, *al-Durr al-muṣān fī sīrat al-Muẓaffar Salīm Khān*, is a panegyric of Sultan Selim after his defeat of the heretical Safavids and the godless Mamluks. It was completed on 10 Ṣafar 926/4 March 1517. Its writer was named 'Alī b. Muḥammad al-Ishbīlī al-Maghribī al-Dimashqī, and, as his name shows, he clearly belonged to a refugee family originating in Seville and coming through north-west Africa before finally taking refuge in Damascus. The writers of these two Arabic tracts evidently saw in Selim the Grim the leader of a *jihād*, a counter-Crusade, who would avenge the wrongs suffered by Muslims at Christian hands. It was ironical that the writer of *al-I'lām* completed his work doubtless unaware that Selim had died on 22 September 1520.

Note

1. al-Nuwayrī al-Iskandarānī, *al-Ilmān*, tr. P. M. Holt.

BIBLIOGRAPHY

Sources available in English translation

A first-hand account of the background and course of the First Crusade by an anonymous Crusader, probably a Norman from southern Italy, is given by Rosalind Hill (ed. and tr.), *Gesta Francorum*, London: Thomas Nelson & Son, 1962. This formed the basis of a work produced early in the twelfth century by a Benedictine monk, Guibert of Nogent, and entitled *Gesta Dei per Francos*, now available in translation by Robert Levine, *The Deeds of God Through the Franks*, Woodbridge: The Boydell Press, 1997. Also valuable is *The First Crusade*, edited with an Introduction by Edward Peters, Philadelphia: University of Pennsylvania Press, 1971. This gives a translation of the chronicle of Fulcher of Chartres and other source materials. The Crusade of King Sigurd is given in Snorri Sturluson, *Heimskringla, Sagas of the Norse Kings*, tr. Samuel Laing, London: Everyman's Library, 1961. The Byzantine view of the First Crusade is presented in E. R. A. Sewter (tr.), *The Alexiad of Anna Comnena*, Harmondsworth: Penguin, 1969. For a contemporary Muslim account, see H. A. R. Gibb (tr.), *The Damascus Chronicle of the Crusades*, London: Luzac & Co., 1967. This consists of the annals from 490/1096 to 555/1160 written by the chronicler Ibn al-Qalānisī in his *Dhayl ta'rīkh Dimashq*, 'The continuation of the chronicle of Damascus'. A later phase of the Crusades is covered by U. and M. C. Lyons with J. S. C. Riley-Smith, *Ayyubids, Mamlukes and Crusaders*, Cambridge: Heffer & Sons, 1971, which contains selections from the chronicle *Ta'rīkh al-duwal wa'l-mulūk*, 'History of the states and kings', of Ibn al-Furāt (d. 807/1405), covering the years 641/1243–4 to 676/1277–8. The translation occupies the second volume of the work.

General histories of the Crusades

Steven Runciman's three-volume work, first published in 1951, *A History of the Crusades*, Harmondsworth: Penguin, is the best-known account in English, and is justly famous for the clarity and elegance of its style. Runciman's access to oriental sources was through translations. A sound single-volume survey is H. E. Mayer, *The Crusades*, tr. J. Gillingham, 2nd edn, Oxford: Oxford University Press, 1988. On a much ampler scale are the volumes of *A History of the Crusades*, published by the University of Wisconsin Press under the general editorship of Kenneth M. Setton. Vol. I: *The First Hundred Years*, ed. Marshall W. Baldwin, and Vol. II: *The Later Crusades, 1189–1311*, eds Robert Lee Wolff and Harry W. Hazard, were both published in 1969. Twelve articles on the Crusades, the Crusaders and the impact on the East, written by leading authorities, have been usefully assembled and reprinted by Thomas F. Madden, *The Crusades: the Essential Readings*, Oxford: Blackwell, 2002. For the cartography of the Muslim world generally, see Hugh Kennedy (ed.), *An Historical Atlas of Islam*, 2nd edn, Leiden: Brill, 2002. Angus Konstam, *Historical Atlas of the Crusades*, Ludlow: Thalamus Publishing, 2002, embodies much illustrated letterpress.

The Crusaders' neighbours in the Near East

A general history of the Byzantine Empire is provided by George Ostrogorsky, *History of the Byzantine State*, tr. Joan Hussey, 2nd edn, Oxford: Blackwell, 1968. J. (Joan) M. Hussey also wrote the relevant chapter, 'The Later Macedonians, the Comneni and the Angeli, 1025–1204' in *The Cambridge Medieval History*, Vol. IV: *The Byzantine Empire and its Neighbours*, Cambridge: Cambridge University Press, 1966. On Armenia in Cilicia (Lesser Armenia) see T. S. R. Boase (ed.), *The Cilician Kingdom of Armenia*, Edinburgh and London: Scottish Academic Press, 1978; Jacob G. Ghazarian, *The Armenian kingdom in Cilicia during the Crusades*, Richmond: Curzon Press, 2000. The history of the Muslim states in this period is surveyed in P. M. Holt, *The Age of the Crusades*, London: Longman, 1986; for greater detail see Nikita Elisséeff, *Nūr ad-Dīn/ Un grand prince musulman de Syrie au temps des Croisades* (3 vols), Damascus: Institut Français de Damas, 1967. A full and balanced treatment of Saladin's career is given in M. C. Lyons and D. E. P. Jackson, *Saladin: The Politics of the Holy War*, Cambridge: Cambridge University Press, 1982. The Muslim view of the Crusades, which tends to be ignored by Western historians, has now been sympathetically presented by Carole Hillenbrand, *The Crusades: Islamic Perspectives*, Edinburgh: Edinburgh University Press, 1999. A useful guide to the rulers and dynasties of this period is provided by C. E. Bosworth, *The New Islamic Dynasties*, Edinburgh: Edinburgh University Press, 1996.

INDEX OF PERSONS

INDEX OF PLACES